BLACK MINDS MATTER

Realizing the Brilliance, Dignity, and Morality of Black Males in Education

J. Luke Wood, Ph.D.

MONTEZUMA PUBLISHING

San Diego, CA

Published by

Montezuma Publishing
Aztec Shops Ltd.
San Diego State University
San Diego, California 92182-1701

619-594-7552

www.montezumapublishing.com

ISBN: 978-0-7442-7494-3

Publishing Manager: Kim Mazyck

Design and Layout: Lia Dearborn

Formatting: Lia Dearborn

Cover Design: Lia Dearborn

Quality Control: Jasmine Baiz

TABLE OF CONTENTS

Black Minds Matter

INSPIRATION AND DEDICATION

I would like to begin this book by acknowledging those who served as the inspiration for this volume. First, this book was inspired by a report that was published by The Education Trust-West called *Black Minds Matter.* This report, released in 2015, examined the experiences and outcomes of Black learners in the State of California. In doing so, the report provided a context for the status of Black learners in the state and a roadmap for educators and policymakers on necessary interventions to improve statewide disparities. Though the report presented data that were California-centric, the patterns identified in student outcomes and recommendations for change bear wider application for addressing disparities facing Black students nationwide.

Another key impetus for this book was Alfred Olango. Alfred was a refugee from Uganda who came to the United States when he was 12 years old. His family was seeking to escape a regime that wanted to kill them. Alfred was a father, a husband, and worked in the food service industry. He hoped to own his own restaurant one day—a dream he was unable to realize. In fall of 2016, Alfred experienced the loss of one of his closest childhood friends. A few days later, his sister noticed that he was not acting like himself and subsequently called the police for help. The police who responded to the scene were not part of the psychiatric response team, though the request his sister made was specifically for this team (K. Davis & Littlefield, 2017). Though he was unarmed, the police mistook a vape smoker in his hand for a gun and shot Alfred at close range, ending his life.

Like so many others before him, Alfred was a Black man who met an untimely end at the hands of those who were sworn to protect him. Immediately following these events, San Diego, CA became engulfed in direct action. Protests, marches, and demonstrations occurred throughout the city, particularly in the El Cajon area where the shooting occurred. Many of the Black doctoral students in the Joint Ph.D. Program in Education between San Diego State University and Claremont Graduate University were involved in these actions. These events spurred an urgency to highlight the parallels between how Black men are criminalized and undervalued in the streets and how these same patterns are manifested in education. As part of that effort, we have sought to acknowledge Alfred's life and memory.

As a result, this book is dedicated to Alfred Olango and his family. It is also dedicated to the brave Ph.D. students who have pushed others, including myself, to more vigorously advocate for positive change in society. This includes Darielle Blevins, Michelle Dejohnette, Sam Scales, Terry Sivers, and James Bolden. And finally, this book is dedicated to Ryan Smith and the rest of The Education Trust-West team who have fought arduously for better policies and decision-making for Black males in society and in education.

A SHORT NOTE

The comments presented in this volume are based on lectures I gave during the Black Minds Matter course and during speeches that were associated with the class. The course was publicly broadcast to over 250 live and replay broadcast sites throughout the nation, with an audience of over 10,000 learners. Writing these ideas down provided an opportunity to more fully convey my perspectives, the extant research, and the necessary path forward for success.

I have purposely written this volume in a conversational tone, with the goal of conveying social science research in a manner that is accessible to the people it is designed to reach. While this volume is designed for educators of Black boys and men, the accessible tone is designed to ensure that the messages expressed are useful for non-educators – namely parents, community members, and advocates for Black males.

The data presented in this volume is derived from a review of extant research as well as my own research findings. In particular, I highlight findings from three guidebooks that are currently being used in the field. These guidebooks include: *Supporting Men of Color in the Community College* (Wood & Harris III, 2017a), *Teaching Men of Color in the Community College* (Wood, Harris III, & White, 2015), and *Teaching Boys and Young Men of Color* (Wood & Harris III, 2017b). The latter two guidebooks were based on studies of promising practices. In Wood et al. (2015), the authors identified college instructors with a documented record of success in teaching men of color. These instructors then completed narratives that offered insight into the practices that they have found to be successful in working with men of color, broadly defined (e..g, Black, Latino, Southeast Asian, Native American, Pacific Islander). The teaching boys of color guidebook (Wood & Harris III, 2017b) adhered to a similar approach, with contributing teachers being nominated by their principals and school heads based on having a documented record of success.

In addition, I have also used new analyses derived from my collaborative research with Idara Essien in the Our Voices project. Our Voices is a national study of cross-racial interactions as documented through the narratives of the parents of Black children. In particular, the study focuses on the experiences that parents and their children have with racial micro-aggressions in early childhood education.

A total of 51 parents contributed counternarratives that illuminated often untold stories. As noted by Solórzano and Yosso (2002), the three main types of counter-stories include personal narratives, other people's narratives, and composite narratives. Personal narratives include researchers offering their own experiences to illuminate patterns of marginalization. Though not directly connected to the our voices project, I have offered my own narratives after each chapter by sharing experiences that directly relate to the chapter themes and content. Other people's narratives include people from marginalized groups sharing their lived experiences. Other people's narratives are included in this volume, as documented from narratives contributed by parents to the Our Voices project. Composite narratives included amalgamated stories that present thematic elements from multiple stories. Composite narratives are particularly useful in portraying common experiences with marginalization, as they synthesize a general experience while also maintaining the anonymity of those who have participated in a study.

Both other people's narratives and composite narratives derived from the aformenetioned studies, particularly from the Our Voices project, are included in this volume. As such, quotes provided in this volume are direct quotes from research or other scholarship; however, quotes denoted with a dagger (†) represent composite narratives. Data from all these projects were all coded using an ideas grouping approach, as espoused by Auerbach and Silverstein (2003). An ideas grouping approach is a modified grounded theory approach that is used for theory generation. The approach involves the identification of recurrent ideas and subjecting these ideas to refinement through constant comparison.

Black Minds Matter

CHAPTER 1

A LETTER ON CIVIL RESISTANCE

Spaces of care have been turned into space of criminalization.
    – Patrisse Cullors (Co-Founder of Black Lives Matter)

Many teachers are sympathetic destroyers of Black boys' dreams.
    – Dr. Tyrone Howard, Professor, UCLA
    (Statements from Black Minds Matter)

In recent years, there have been many high-profile slayings of young Black men: Trayvon Martin, Michael Brown, Tamir Rice, Eric Garner, Stephon Clark, Alfred Olango, and far too many others. Anger in response to these slayings has led to numerous marches, protests, and vigils throughout the nation. Rising through the power of social media, the Black Lives Matter movement has shed light on the injustices facing Black communities and has provided a statement of affirmation that Black lives do indeed matter.

Shadowing this movement, there has been increased discourse about the status, experiences, and outcomes of Black students in education, particularly Black males. Black Lives Matter has shown that Black boys and men are devalued and overcriminalized in society. These same patterns are evident in educational settings, leading to overrepresentation in special education, exposure to high rates of suspension and expulsion, and ultimately, feeding the school-to-prison pipeline. Similar disparities are manifested in college and university settings (Howard, 2013b; Wood, 2017).

As such, there remains a need to increase the national consciousness about issues facing Black boys and men in education. This volume seeks to support that aim, by drawing parallels between issues Black males face in society and the ways that Black minds are engaged in the classroom. Through this lens, this volume will synthesize research that can benefit Black males at all levels of education, from preschool to doctoral levels, emphasizing strategies and practices to support their success.

This volume is an outgrowth of comments that my colleagues and I made during the Black Minds Matter public course that was nationally streamed in Fall 2017. Black Minds Matter is an adjoining movement to the Black Lives Matter movement that provides an affirmative statement that Black minds do matter. This movement began in 2015 as an outgrowth of a widely heralded policy report released by The Education Trust-West titled *Black Minds Matter* and has manifested through numerous symposia, convenings, articles, scholarly talks, and the Black Minds course. In general, these efforts are guided by the tenets, critique, and sensemaking of the Black Lives Matter movement. Specifically, the Black Lives Matter movement's guiding tenets of loving engagement, collective value, and restorative justice serve as a framework for Black Minds advocates who seek to enhance outcomes for Black learners in education.

Civil Resistance in the Classroom

As a Black Minds advocate, I encourage educators to embrace the philosophy of civil resistance in the classroom. Civil resistance is a strategy of nonviolent action where coordinated efforts are taken to undermine and resist an oppressive source of power. This source of power is often represented by a class of people, an unjust policy, or a social structure the reifies privilege and advantage for some by way of marginalizing and disadvantaging others (Chenoweth, 2014). Inevitably, those in power seek to maintain and extend their power (Delgado & Stefancic, 2017), rationalizing their actions as moral, all the while fearful of a world that would render them without the same opportunities they have withheld from others.

The tools that a civil resistance uses to confront this power are peaceful actions, such as protests, boycotts, sit-ins, vigils, demonstrations, and other similar strategies. These acts meet violence with nonviolence, hate with love. Throughout our nation's history, people have engaged in various forms of collective action. Civil resistance was expressed in many forms during the Civil Rights Movement, the Black Power Movement, and now through Black Lives Matter. And, some progress has been realized. We have experienced successes, such as ending miscegenation laws and Jim Crow, but we have faced numerous defeats, none more palpable than the inability to change a culture that is rooted and fertilized by racism.

While old trees have fallen, and new trees have grown, the problem of racism persists because the soil—our culture—has never changed. As we pass from one generation to the next, the distance between slavery, overt racism, and ourselves grows farther, yet our understanding of how we are all connected to the peculiar institution (slavery) that ripped son from mother, daughter from father, loved one from the loved, and sold them into bondage, fades. Time passes, and these faded memories further spur our culture of racism because we begin to rationalize illegitimate notions as simply "the way we operate" and "the way we have always done it."

But, ultimately, when we trace back why certain practices exist, why certain policies are in place, we find a glaring truth. This culture permeates all of our social institutions and is chiefly promulgated in our nation's schools, colleges, and universities. We can further this understanding by examining who benefits from this culture, as it is not by accident that our educational institutions produce certain outcomes for some people and other outcomes for others. As W. Edward Deming noted, "Every system is perfectly designed to achieve the results that it gets," and a culture of racism and a history of slavery inform our social systems—the ways our schools teach, our hospitals care, our courtrooms rule. Thus, every system is perfectly designed to accomplish one goal: to perpetuate disparities, and to serve as engines of social reproduction.

Halting these engines is no easy task because humankind has a tendency to do harm to others. Moreover, we have not been as strategic as we could be in doing so—we have not truly addressed the engine. Eric Bishop, a leading college administrator, once said, "We have to stop shifting sand and get to the bedrock" (personal communication, July 20, 2017). By shifting sand, he means that, too often, we focus on issues that are important but never dig deep beneath the sand to address the bedrock—the fact that our schooling systems are chief drivers of our divisive culture. These systems are designed to produce a society of haves and have-nots, and to a marvelous degree of accuracy, they succeed in doing so.

There is an old adage that "the pen is mightier than the sword." This is true because of the power of ideas. An idea can spark a movement, overthrow a government, and disempower a tyrant. This is why dictators burn books, manuscripts, and other records—

because of the salience and threat that ideas possess. Words and ideas have the power to subjugate and to empower. In our classrooms, they do both simultaneously, so much so that I remain in awe. I awe not at the beauty of the system, as there is nothing beautiful about oppression. I am in awe of how the system can place two children of different racial backgrounds in the exact same classroom and produce two very different experiences and outcomes—at the exact same time.

As an educator, I truly believe in the power of the pen. But, borrowing from this metaphor of weaponry, I also believe, while the "pen is mightier than the sword," "the classroom is more powerful than the catapult." The classroom is *the* central public domain through which ideas are expressed to children, where values are affirmed, where assumptions are conveyed as truth, where the written text is analyzed and studied. This is why the classroom is so powerful, because it is the primary site for public socialization to American life. Therefore, the classroom must be the central site of a civil resistance, because for our Black boys and men, it is a site where dreams are stolen, where disassociation with school is manifested, and where the chains of imprisonment are tightened slowly—tighter and tighter until one's mind is taught to extol the captors and embrace a second-class status.

Our Black males do not enter a domain that represents their community. The textbooks that are used, the authors that are esteemed, the art on the walls, and the ideas that are embraced are those that emanate from a system that sustains itself by requiring the participation of Black males as "workers," members of the "underclass," and "prisoners." This occurs through an education that commits daily violence toward them by devaluing their minds, criminalizing their actions, and withholding messages that can liberate them. As wisely stated by Bush and Bush (2013), Black males do not reject education; rather, they thirst for knowledge and fight to learn. What they reject are schooling practices that maintain and continue asymmetrical power relations. They reject an education that simultaneously and marvelously prepares others to be "leaders," members of the "ruling class," and owners of production.

Given that education is the primary domain by which our culture is continued, it is essential that educators begin to embrace a paradigm shift that radically reconsiders their role in education, seeing their classrooms, offices, and schoolyards as sites for civil resistance. And, we must resist. To see school as a site for civil resistance means embracing a calling and a life purpose that advances light in a system of darkness. And, make no mistake, our resistance will be a long, arduous struggle. For we struggle not against people, or buildings, or even practices, but their source of power—our culture. And in our current era, the darkness seems darker now than it has seemed for a long time. But, the light is always the brightest when it is darkest, and to be a light is to embrace civil resistance in the classroom.

Our struggle is likely one that we will never fully win, at least not in our own lifetimes, but struggle we must, as our forbearers did, incrementally creating a better world for the next generation. Educators of all racial backgrounds must embrace this ideology, offering light through civil resistance. While there are many forms of civil resistance, in an educational setting, there is nothing more powerful than an art of teaching that empowers those who have been downtrodden by society—those who have been systematically disaffected, minoritized, and targeted. A civil resistance that seeks to bring light to the educational system is one that prioritizes empowerment. It is one that embraces a new educational paradigm that truly values the intelligence, worth, and morality of Black minds.

We must be clear about what we are resisting. We are resisting explicit bias, unconscious bias, stereotypes, and microaggressions. We are resisting school tracking and the school-to-prison pipeline. We are resisting overplacement in special education and overexposure to exclusionary discipline, such as suspensions and expulsion. We are resisting a marginalizing curriculum that mars our students' prospects and dreams. In an educational setting, a civil resistance is most impactful through teaching that empowers the disaffected. Thus, a civil resistance is guided not by hate, but by love. To truly empower, one must communicate resistance through love. This is why a civil resistance is peaceful. The late Asa Hilliard wrote:

I have never encountered any children in any group who are not geniuses.

There is no mystery on how to teach them. The first thing you do is treat them like human beings and the second thing you do is love them.

Bringing love into the educational system involves embracing a new educational paradigm that truly values the intelligence, worth, and morality of Black minds. As a person of faith, my approach to civil resistance is rooted in the adage, "Love your neighbor as yourself" (Mark 12:31). As educators, we have the privilege of educating our neighbors and the children of our neighbors. Therefore, we must embrace their children, not as strangers, but as our own. Informed by this perspective, I believe we can apply this view to the educational experiences of our Black boys and men. The path forward involves the following principle: Love your neighbor as yourself, and love their children as your children. Teach them with love, discipline them with love, build personal relationships with love—as if they were your own. Some refer to this as an emancipatory pedagogy, a liberatory pedagogy, or a critical pedagogy. We can embrace the spirit of all these notions, as well as an unapologetically Black ideology that is grounded in resistance, and we can construct a Black Minds Pedagogy, a pedagogy of love to confront a system that permeates racism, supremacy, and dehumanization.

Personal Story – Academic Activism

Academic activism is at the center of this book and my life. The work I do is designed to create a better future for our Black boys and men. The spark for this commitment was lit early in my academic career, while I was still an undergraduate. During my senior year and after years of advocating for Black student retention, I began to read literature on how the presence of faculty and administrators of color could enable the success of students of color. Simultaneously, the Black student leaders and I noticed that there was a dwindling number of Black faculty and administrators on our campus, and with every retirement or resignation, there was a permanent loss as their replacements were primarily non-Black.

In 2005, three other students and I spearheaded a group that organized Black faculty, staff, students, and community members to advocate for improved conditions for African Americans on campus. The initiative was spearheaded out of our roles in student government and as campus student organization leaders. After a series of meetings, our group presented the President of the University with a proposal that outlined problems of academic and professional success for Black students, faculty, and administrators on campus. We wrote the following:

Proposal to President for African American Affirmative Action

The students desire more ethnic diversity in the campus faculty/staff and administration. This is our plan for Affirmative Action.

Problem:

The student body is composed 44% White, 17% Asian, 14% Hispanic, 6% African American, 3% Foreign, 1% Native American, and 16% Other. However, the diversity breakdown of the faculty is not in alignment with these numbers. White professors are overrepresented and African Americans are underrepresented. 75.6% of the faculty are White, while only 4.3% are Black. This is overtly apparent in these colleges:

- Arts and Letters – 84.7% White and 2.7% Black
- Business Administration – 73.5% White and 1% Black
- Natural Sciences – 82.3% White and 1.8% Black

We believe that one cause for high student attrition rates is students' comfort with the climate on campus. Only 17% of African Americans who enter as a first-time freshman will graduate in a 5-year timespan, while 37% of Whites graduate in that same time period. In the aforementioned colleges, student graduation rates are especially low, and we believe this is in connection to the number of faculty in the college that students have to identify with. For instance, in the College of Business Administration, only 10% of African Americans who enter as first-time freshman will graduate in a 5-year timespan.

In response to these conditions, we requested that specific action be taken. These included: (a) hiring or elevating an African American administrator to serve on the university's Executive Committee; (b) transitioning an African American dean from an interim to a permanent placement; (c) issuing an executive memorandum to hiring committees that informed search committees that candidate pools would not be certified unless there was sufficient diversity in the applications; (d) hiring a Black male administrator to address affirmative action issues in hiring; and (e) allocating funds to support ongoing Black student retention efforts.

After sending our proposal to the President, our group coordinated a meeting with him to lobby for our requests. It is important to note that the focus of our efforts was the retention of African American faculty and administrators, as our proposal arose out of a recent firing of an African American Associate Vice President. This former Associate Vice President had been the most recent among a group of six other African American upper-level administrators who had been fired or forced to resign between the early to mid-2000s. In fact, with her firing, only two Black executive-level administrators remained on campus.

After the meeting, we had individuals from throughout the community—including local political leaders—contact the President to state their support of our efforts. During a follow-up meeting with our group, the President stated that finding Black administrators and faculty was nearly impossible, because the market was too competitive to hire them. At the meeting, we offered the names of Black leaders who could serve as Dean. The President stated that he did not believe they were qualified, but stated, "You're welcome to take the applications and render a recommendation. You can get them from the Vice President for Academic Affairs office" (this Vice President was also in attendance at the meeting).

The next day, the administrator in charge of the documents called me to "come and pick up the applications at 1:00 p.m." I did not pick the applications up that day, but the next day, I called her to let her know I was coming to pick up the documents. When I arrived, the administrator with whom I had spoken on the phone was out to lunch, but her student assistant gave me an envelope with the materials. I reviewed the documents with the other Black student leaders and then returned them within the hour. Two weeks later, as I was exiting class, a student affairs administrator met me outside to hand me a letter. The letter stated that I was being accused of stealing documents from the Vice President's Office. These documents were the candidate files that I had returned a couple weeks prior, along with our recommendations, per the President's permission.

The letter noted that I could either take 1-year probation with a flag placed on my permanent file or fight the charges and face long-term suspension/expulsion. Both of the other student leaders also received letters that same day. One of my faculty mentors immediately placed me in contact with a lawyer from the National Association for the Advancement of Colored People (NAACP). They secured a lawyer for me who volunteered for both the NAACP and the American Civil Liberties Union (ACLU). Over the next 6 months, I met regularly with these lawyers as they began to build my defense. I developed a close relationship with them and learned about broader issues of injustice they were engaged in across the region.

I was fortunate at that time to have an African American state assembly member in my corner—the late Mervyn Dymally. Mervyn was a friend of my boss and also served on the legislative higher education finance subcommittee. Once he learned of the issue, he made a number of phone calls to the college President asking him to relent on his charges. An acquaintance of mine who worked in the Governor's Office also made several phone calls and placed additional pressure on the President. Despite the mounting political pressure, the President pressed forward with his efforts to remove me from campus.

It was 6 months between the time I received the note and when my hearing occurred. In the time between, my friendships and associations on campus dwindled. I noticed that other students who had long fought beside me avoided being seen with me on campus. It was like I was a dead man walking. This was not only restricted to other students. In fact, a faculty member with whom I was very close was noticeably avoidant. He was someone who I looked up to, and this was a period of time when I needed friends to rally behind me, but he was absent. He was the faculty advisor for my student organization and was a former member of the Black Panthers. One day, I saw him on campus, and as I walked up to him, he looked around to see who else was watching us. He turned to me and said, "Luke, the block is too hot around you right now. I can't be seen with you." In total disbelief, I remember asking him if he was serious. He said, "Yes." I was most surprised because the professor was a former Panther and fashioned himself as an activist-leader, but it turned out he was not. During that time, I learned who my real friends were. It was an important message in humility and trust.

The Chief Judicial Officer assigned to the case was named Sarah. Sarah was a Nigerian American and a former NAACP chapter president. She began the diligent process of putting together the campus' case against me. She collected data from the involved students, conducted interviews with campus administrators, and gathered all available documentation. Early on, Sarah recognized that the administration's case did not quite "add up." Moreover, in private conversations with Black faculty on campus, she was learning that the sequence of events suggested that the students had been "set-up" in retaliation for bringing a negative light to the campus. Despite data that seemed to indirectly support this assertion, Sarah pressed forward. About a week before the case was set for a hearing, Sarah had a conversation with an executive administrator that confirmed her suspicions. He told her that he disagreed with the case, noting that he felt conflicted because he had been complicit in the President's effort to set us up and felt poorly about his decision to go along with the President's actions. He noted having a conversation with the President the day before I was given the documents where the President discussed his dislike for me and stated that he was going to play "hard ball" with me. Now, Sarah was placed in the same difficult position, having to determine whether or not she would also go along with the President's efforts to retaliate.

The days leading up to the trial were nerve racking for me. I knew that the truth was on my side, but nothing more. I woke up the morning of the hearing prepared mentally for battle. I knew they would try to ask me questions in ways that would place me on the defensive, and that I needed to stay calm. As I was on my way to the hearing, I received a frantic phone call from my lawyer. He said, "Luke, Luke, come to the office quick! There is no hearing today— come quick! It was Sarah." I drove as fast as I could to the office. When I walked in, they gleefully greeted me and handed me a letter, but before I had a chance to read it, they told me what had happened. They noted that, earlier that same morning, Sarah had submitted a letter of resignation to the campus, indicating that she would no longer be serving as the Chief Judicial Officer. I was startled, and I said, "What's does that mean? Does this mean they are trying the case at a later point once they get a new person in place?" They responded, "No. Sarah resigned and then she called us to have us add her as a witness for *our* side for the hearing. When we submitted the name addition to the university this morning we immediately received as response saying, All charges have been dropped, and you are free to carry on with your studies." I was overcome with emotion—after 6 months of believing I might lose my academic career, my case was dropped.

Several years later, long after I had graduated with my bachelor's and earned my master's, I ran into one of the executive leaders on campus who had been intimately involved with leading the charge against me. He pulled me aside at a conference and told me that he wanted to apologize to me. I asked him why. He noted that he was now separated from the university. He also stated that he felt bad about what he and others had been complicit in. It was a heartfelt apology with full acknowledgement of the toll that it had placed on me. I forgave him. But, in some respects, I could have thanked him. What they intended to make happen turned out to be good, as I have been a dedicated advocate for Black student success ever since, and the event only served to strengthen me and my life's purpose in this respect.

Names have been replaced with pseudonyms.

Black Minds Matter

16

CHAPTER 2

POLICING BLACK LIVES, SCHOOLING BLACK MINDS

We must make sure that schools are enacting alternatives to punitive discipline.

– Pedro Noguera, Professor, UCLA
(Statement from Black Minds Matter)

In this chapter, I will discuss the importance of linking Black lives and Black minds. To do so, I will explore patterns in policing that are also evident in schooling that similarly devalue and criminalize Black males. The goal is to demonstrate that educators cannot discuss Black minds if we do not value Black lives, because Black lives and Black minds are inextricably intertwined, for if one does not value life, then they certainly cannot value the mind. In a society that constantly devalues the very being of one group of people, it is hard to urge those who are responsible for educating them to prioritize their minds. The hard truth is this: Names such as Trayvon Martin, Michael Brown, Tamir Rice, Eric Garner, Stephon Clark, and Alfred Olango represent the criticality of affirming Black lives. Their stories readily serve to demonstrate how Black lives are undervalued and criminalized. And, there are thousands of Trayvons, Tamirs, and Erics who traverse our classrooms every day who face "real" and "symbolic" violence. Their stories similarly demonstrate how Black minds are undervalued and criminalized in education.

This point became most apparent to me after reading Tyrone Howard's (2016) article, "Why Black Lives (and Minds) Matter." Howard, a nationally renowned Professor at UCLA, was one of the first authors I read who made such a clear linkage between Black lives and Black minds. In this article, he argued that linking these two concepts is essential because of "persistent and seemingly unchanging data" that demonstrate the inadequate education that Black boys and men receive. This is inclusive of data on the poor outcomes for Black boys and men across the educational pipeline, and the "brazen indifference," "direct violence," "scrutiny," and "criminalization" against Black boys and men that has "become normalized" in our nation's schools, colleges, and universities (Howard, 2016). Indeed, direct violence and symbolic violence against Black boys and men has become so pervasive that it is normalized.

From a critical race theory perspective, the word "normal" has a salient connotation. Normal refers to the everyday racialized experiences faced by communities of color. These experiences are enduring. Normal does not have a positive value connotation associated with it—that is, normal does not mean "good" (Delgado & Stefancic, 2017). It is simply normal. Consider the power of this statement: The criminalization of Black learners is normal. Howard (2016) noted that schools with high concentrations of Black learners engage them as criminals when they walk through the door. They enter the building through metal detectors. They walk down hallways passing by police officers, school resource officers, and private security guards. They are under video surveillance that tracks their movements and they are subjected to randomized checks for drugs, guns, and other illicit materials. In the United States, many schools now operate like prisons, preparing some for college and the workforce and others for prison. Given this, Howard (2016) contends that affirming Black lives and Black minds is necessary for reclaiming the "humanity and dignity" of Black learners that is not evident in educational settings.

Honestly addressing the pervasive criminalization of Black minds requires an understanding of how these patterns are cultivated. As noted earlier, the soil—our culture—is rooted in notions of racism, supremacy, and dehumanization. All societies socialize individuals to accept notions that certain groups of people have more value than others. In the United States, this is chiefly manifested through the lens of racism, where people of color are viewed as having less worth than others. As a result, Black people are dehumanized, being perceived as less than human, and in some cases, viewed as having no worth at all. This soil fertilizes the roots of all our social systems (e.g., health care, education, law enforcement, industry). This leads to the ubiquitous undervaluing and criminalizing of Black lives and Black minds.

These viewpoints of these social systems influence all aspects of the Black experience. In policing, this has resulted in Black people being more likely to be subjected to the use of deadly force, excessive force, racial profiling, and other ills. In education, undervaluing and criminalization have led to equivalent practices, such as excessive suspensions and expulsions, overplacement in special education, and a proliferation of zero tolerance policies. The similarities found between the main social systems in our culture fall into three primary categories: *assumed aberrance, aggressive policing,* and *racial profiling*. These three categoires will be discussed in greater depth in the following sections.

Assumed Aberrance

Assumed aberrance refers to widely held perspectives about Black males that assume they are inherently devious and disobedient. As a result of these perspectives, aggressive policing practices are enacted that are designed to contain, control, and render Black males powerless. Doing so requires racial profiling practices that identify and target Black people. Black men are assumed to be aberrant, having innate qualities that are bad. This is manifested in policing and schooling that engages Black males as if they are hypercriminalized "beasts of prey." In response, many law enforcement officers and educators engage Black males with a battle zone mentality that demonstrates a blatant disregard for their youthfulness. Table 1 demonstrates the language used to refer to these concepts in both schooling and policing.

Table 1

Assumed Aberrance

Concept	Policing	Schooling
Beasts of Prey	Super Predators	Super Threats
Hypercriminalized	Overexposed to Criminal (In)Justice System	Overexposed to Exclusionary Discipline
Battle Zone Mentality	Warrior Mindset	Principal Effect
Disregard of Youthfulness	Treated as Adults	Denial of Innocence

Beasts of Prey

As a result of the pervasive dehumanization of Black boys and men, they are viewed through the lens of "beasts of prey." This image has its origins in the 1915 movie, *Birth of a Nation,* directed by D. W. Griffith. The movie was based on the 1905 novel, *The Clansman,* and aggressively portrays Black men as lazy, sex-crazed rapists, and brutalizers (Dixon, 1905). One of the most infamous scenes from the movie is a deranged emancipated slave chasing his former White mistress after she declines his proposal for marriage. She ends the chase by throwing herself off of a cliff to her death to avoid being brutalized by him. The film depicts her brother as founding the Ku Klux Klan to protect innocent Whites from "demonic Black males." The film led to the resurgence of the Klan in the United States, which reached its peak in membership only a decade after the film's release. The image of Black males proffered in *Birth of a Nation* still resides within the national psyche of Americans, as it has been repeatedly reintroduced to audiences through television and the media ever since. In the policing and schooling of Black males, this notion of them being seen as beasts of prey is evident.

As beasts of prey, Black boys and men are viewed as "super predators" in policing and as "super threats" in schooling. The concept of the super predator became part of the common lexicon in the 1990s. Largely, this is due to the ideas offered by political scientist, John Dilulio (1995). During the Clinton Administration, Dilulio visited the White House and extended his sensemaking around Black criminality to the Clinton Administration. President Clinton was very interested in Dilulio's perspective. Dilulio (1995) later shared his sentiments in an opinion editorial in *The Weekly Standard*:

> They kill or maim on impulse, without any intelligible motive . . . the buzz of impulsive violence, the vacant stares and smiles, and the remorseless eyes . . . they quite literally have no concept of the future . . . they place zero value on the lives of their victims, whom they reflexively dehumanize . . . capable of committing the most heinous acts of physical violence for the most trivial reasons. (para. 4)

These words do not sound like someone who is talking about people, but rather an animal—a super predator. These words align with the animalistic portrayal of Black men as articulated in *Birth of a Nation*. The Clinton Administration embraced these ideas, extending a crime bill that criminalized Black and Brown communities and destroyed countless families. In touting the benefits of the bill, Hillary Clinton (1996) stated:

> . . . they are not just gangs of kids anymore, they are often the kinds of kids that are called super predators. No conscience. No empathy. We can talk about why they ended up that way but first we need to bring them to heel.

This language mirrors that of Dilulio's and demonstrates how the racist ideology of one person served to influence an administration, similar to how Griffith's films accomplished the same end 80 years earlier. Similar framing is seen in how Black males are depicted in the media in recent years—for example, in the case of Michael Brown. Darren Wilson, the officer who shot Brown, was reported to have described Brown as "aggressive, angry and like a demon just moments before he ended the 18-year-old's life" (as cited in Hackman, 2016, para. 31).

The description of Black learners as super predators was connected to the notion of super-predators early on. In the same article, Dilulio (1995) highlights the comments of Lynne Abraham who he described as a "no-nonsense" district attorney:

> We're talking about boys whose voices have yet to change. We're talking about elementary school youngsters who pack guns instead of lunches. We're talking about kids who have absolutely no respect for human life and no sense of the future. In short, we're talking about big trouble that hasn't yet begun to crest. And make no mistake, while the trouble will be greatest in Black inner-city neighborhoods, other places are also certain to have burgeoning youth-crime problems that will spill over into upscale central-city districts, inner-ring suburbs, and even the rural heartland. (para. 2)

The notion of being beasts of prey does not end in policing; there are similar ways that this manifests in education. In particular, educators often use similar descriptions of Black boys and men, referring to them as "combative," "deviant," "defiant," "thugs," "confrontational," "aggressive," "violent," "disruptive," "delinquents," "gangsters," and "troublemakers" (Harper & Wood, 2015; Howard, 2013a; Noguera, 2003). Clearly, this language does not sound like descriptions of learners. However, while educators often use this type of language, the vast majority of educators do not believe that they might tacitly ascribe to racist ideologies. This is because the vast majority of educators are good people who are well-meaning and who want to do the right thing. But, we are all socialized in the same society that has routinely depicted Black boys and men in a criminalized fashion, and so educators buy into these notions and subsequently engage with Black males through this lens (Noguera, 2003).

A common way that this issue is seen in community colleges is in the "subtle step back." This refers to stepping back or distancing ourselves from someone because we perceive them, unconsciously, to be a threat. For instance, let's say a class has just ended and some students are filing out of the door while others are approaching the professor to have questions asked. While this is occurring, a Black male student approaches the professor on the periphery, and the professor only gets a glancing eye view of him. The professor's natural reaction might be to step back, even slightly, because the professor has been taught throughout their life to fear him. In that moment, the educator has communicated to the student that they fear him. This is challenging because educators cannot teach someone who they fear, as it will mar the interactions they have with the student. Typically, a common response is for educators to recognize that they have communicated a slight and to step forward, put their hands in a welcoming position, smile, and say something positive. But, even in that moment, their actions only serve to further make clear that the unintended was actually intended (Wood, Harris III, & White, 2015). Another example of perceiving Black men as beasts of prey comes from Solórzano, Ceja, and Yosso's (2000) research. Here is a quote from a student in their study on racial microaggressions:

> It's 11 o'clock [at night] and all of a sudden [campus police] sweeps up . . . there's a total of four or five cars, and then we have two cops on the bikes, all here for us who are not displaying any type of violence or anything like that . . .

but we're upset. And, we're saying at the same time, we're feeling restricted because if we act in a way that we want to react, number one, we're going to go to jail; number two, it's just going to feed into the stereotype that we're supposed to be violent. . . . We actually just stood out there and just pleaded our case for at least a good 45 minutes. And they were not trying to hear us at all. We had to leave the parking lot. . . . Once again, it reminded me I'm a Black man [on a predominantly White campus]. (p. 69)

Battle Zone Mentality

Another example of assumed aberrance is being treated by educators with a battle zone mentality. A battle zone is a locale where individuals are engaged in battle, a soldier warring against enemy combatants. The sensemaking behind a battle zone mentality is that if a police officer or educator is engaging someone who is potentially violent, or someone of whom they should be fearful, then the environment they are in is no longer "normal," but has become a battle zone. In that battle zone, the perspective is that you must engage your adversary with that context in mind (Modell & Cropp, 2007).

In policing, there are two different mindsets that are discussed related to how officers approach their work. The first is having a warrior mindset, where they perceive they are going to war. This is the manifestation of a battle zone mentality in policing. From this perspective, their job is to "bust down doors," "get the bad guys," and "bring down the criminals." The second perspective is that of a guardian mindset, where their role is to protect and serve. A guardian sees their chief role as building relationships, being involved in the community, and protecting their people—not going to war. There are good police officers and bad police officers, just as there are good educators and bad educators. The reality is, the vast majority of police officers and educators do not fall into either of these categories, but instead fall somewhere in the middle. They are, more often than not, people with good intentions who do not realize their unconscious biases and, therefore, cause harm. Our popular media glorifies police officers with a warrior mindset—this is reinforced in film. According to Roufa (2018), the warrior mindset is common. He stated:

> We train our police officers to be warriors, to be ready to face any fight and engage nearly any threat. Our officers stand on the thin blue line . . . a battle line we have drawn between law abiding citizens and the criminals. (para. 2)

The battle zone mentality plays out in educational settings through what we refer to as the "principal effect." When I grew up, I watched numerous films that all had similar depictions of urban schools, Black males, and the educators who were there to "clean them up." Hollywood has long depicted urban schools as war zones and men of color as dangerous adversaries that require school educators and leaders to engage them in battle to "save" the school from further deterioration. There are numerous examples of this, such as the movies *One Eight Seven*, *The Principal*, and *The Substitute*. In particular, *The Principal* serves as the clearest example of this theme, portraying urban schools as war zones where teachers must battle dangerous adversaries—their students. Interestingly, my identical twin brother was in the movie. He played the young son of a teen mother who attended the school. In this movie, a reject teacher named Rick Latimer (who is a drunk and a sexist) is tagged with becoming

Brandel High's principal. The school is depicted as dilapidated and infested with drugs, gangs, and a culture of crime and disrespect. The villain in the film is a gang leader named Victor Duncan who leads many of the illicit activities at the school and threatens Latimer with a knife. Movies like *The Principal* rest within the national psyche of school educators, repeatedly being recast, revised, and replayed before audiences that buy into their racist depictions of Black boys and men. These depictions are replayed every day in the lives and experiences of Black students.

Hypercriminalization

The next theme that is evident in the policing and schooling of Black boys and men is hypercriminalization. It is widely known that Black men are overexposed to the criminal (in)justice system. I use the term (in)justice because, oftentimes, there is no justice within the system. In fact, one of the most searing poems by Langston Hughes critiqued the image of Lady Justice, who is blindfolded and holding the two ends of a scale to demonstrate that justice should be fairly applied. He said, "That justice is a blind goddess is a thing to which we black are wise. Her bandage hides two festering sores that once perhaps were eyes" (Hughes, 1967, p. 45). In 2008, The Pew Charitable Trust released a report titled, *One in 100: Behind Bars in America 2009*, that examined the overrepresentation of people of color in the criminal (in)justice system. They found that among White men who were 18 years of age or older, 1 in 106 were behind bars. In comparison, 1 in 36 Hispanic/Latino men within this same age range were behind bars. While the comparison between Whites and Hispanics demonstrates a significant disparity, even more glaring was the fact that 1 in 15 Black men who were 18 years of age or older were behind bars. The report also found that there were certain age ranges where this disparity was even greater. For instance, among those 20 to 34 years of age, 1 in every 9 Black men were behind bars. Data from 2013 helped to demonstrate the permanence of this pattern. According to The Sentencing Project (2013), "One of every three black American males born today can expect to go to prison in his lifetime . . . compared to one of every seventeen white males" (p. 1).

The same pattern is evident in education. While hypercriminalization results in overexposure to the criminal (in) justice system, it also results in overexposure to exclusionary discipline. Exclusionary discipline refers to practices that exclude students from learning environments. This can involve removing students from the classroom (short-term suspensions), in-house suspensions, out-of-school suspensions, and expulsions (Wood, Harris III, & Howard, 2018). In fact, Black students are significantly more likely to be exposed to exclusionary discipline. This pattern begins early in their educational experiences—in preschool. For example, while Black learners account for 18% of students in preschool, they represent 42% of students who receive out-of-school suspensions. Even more, they account for 48% of students who receive multiple out-of-school suspensions—again, in preschool. In contrast, White students account for 43% of students in preschool, but only 28% of those who received out-of-school suspensions or 26% of those who received multiple out-of-school suspensions (U.S. Office of Civil Rights, 2014b). The pattern that begins in preschool continues through students' educational experiences. From kindergarten through high school, Black learners account for 16% of enrolled students but represent 32% of those who receive in-school suspensions, 33% of those who receive out-of-school suspensions, 42% of those who receive multiple out-of-school suspensions, and 34% of those who are expelled. This significant overrepresentation is juxtaposed with the lack of exposure to exclusionary discipline among their White peers (U.S. Office of Civil Rights, 2014a).

Beyond this, it is also true that Black students who have disabilities are treated with greater hypercriminality and viciousness than their peers. First, it is important to recognize that Black boys are overrepresented in special education (J. E. Davis, 2003; Noguera 2003)—often because educators simply do not believe in their capacity to learn and do not know what "to do with them." Special education can be truly beneficial for students who actually need it, but it has become a dumping ground for Black boys. For example, data from the U.S. Office of Civil Rights (2014b) demonstrated that Black children account for 19% of students with disabilities. However, they represent 36% of students with disabilities who are subject to restraint by a mechanical device. This involves a physical device that is used to prevent them from moving—again, these are children with disabilities.

Disregard for Youthfulness

Recognizing that Black boys and men are viewed as beasts of prey, are hypercriminalized, and are treated by educators as though they are in a battle zone, then it should not be surprising that dehumanization prevents Black children from being children. In our society, there is a blatant and ubiquitous disregard for Black youthfulness (sometimes referred to as adultification; see Ferguson, 2010). The qualities of being children are not readily extended to

29

Black children—this occurs in policing and in schooling. In policing, Black children are perceived and treated as adults. For example, Goff, Jackson, Di Leone, Culotta, and DiTomasso (2014) conducted a study using data from 60 police officers from a large urban police department. They presented the officers with scenarios read cases with different key suspects in mind. These cases were broken down into misdemeanor and felony cases. The officers had to estimate the age of the youth involved, as guided by each scenario. What they found was that, for misdemeanor cases, White suspects' ages were slightly overestimated by about half a year. In contrast, Black suspects were assumed to be 2.5 years older than they actually were. The difference was even greater with felony cases. For felony cases, White ages were underestimated by almost a year, while Black suspects' ages were overestimated by 4.5 years. Given this, it is perceived that Black youth are viewed as being older than they actually are, taking away their youth. Similar patterns are seen among Black youth who are serving life without the possibility of parole for nonviolent offenses. According to the ACLU (2014a), Black youth account for 60% of those who are serving life terms for nonviolent crimes. In stark contrast, Whites account for approximately 15% of youth serving these same types of sentences.

The manifestation of treating Black males as adults was also evident in the Trayvon Martin and Tamir Rice cases. With respect to the slaying of Trayvon Martin:

> George Zimmerman admitted at his 2012 bail hearing that he misjudged Trayvon Martin's age when he killed him. "I though he was a little bit younger than I am," he said,

meaning just under 28. But Trayvon was only 17. (Bernstein, 2017, para. 1)

In terms of Tamir Rice, a young child who was shot by police for having a toy gun, the same pattern is evident. One news article noted the following:

> In statements released Tuesday, the two Cleveland police officers involved in the shooting death of 12-year-old Tamir Rice said that they believed the boy was much older than he was and that Tamir reached for the toy weapon tucked in his waistband before one of the officers opened fire. (Lowery & Scruggs, 2015, para. 1)

As demonstrated in both cases, the byproduct of being criminalized and treated as adults has fatal implications for Black boys.

Black boys are treated as older even in the court system. For example, according to the California Department of Justice (2014), Black youth account for 27% of all direct file cases for a minor who is immediately brought to adult court. These are cases that are immediately elevated to adult courts. Moreover, they account for 24.3% of cases that are reviewed and then transferred to an adult court. In comparison, White defendants account for only 10.3% of direct file and 9.4% of transfer cases. The outgrowth of having a case brought to adult court is that those charged with crimes are going to prison. For instance, 89% of cases involving Black youth that are tried in adult court will result in a conviction, compared to 76% of cases for White youth.

The disregard of youthfulness seen in policing is also evident in education, referred to as a *denial of innocence*. Ladson-Billings

(2011) discussed this pattern in her article, "Boyz to Men." She stated:

> The paradox of Black boys' experiences in school and society is that mainstream perceptions of them vacillate between making them babies and making them men. . . . Their childhood evaporates before they are eight or nine-years-old when teachers and their school officials begin to think of them as "men" . . . the once "cute" boys become problematic "men." (Ladson-Billings, 2011, p. 10)

Goff et al.'s (2014) research supported Ladson-Billings' insights. In Goff et al.'s study, students attending a large, public university were given descriptions of different scenarios involving children and asked to rate the degree to which they thought the child was innocent. They divided the rating into age ranges so comparisons could be made across race and age groups. They found that there was no significant difference between Black and White children between the ages of 0 to 4 or between the ages of 5 to 9. However, at 10 to 13 years of age, the innocence ratings of Black children and White children are viewed differently. At this age, Black children are perceived to be significantly less innocent than their peers, a pattern that continued across all other age groups in the study.

Combining the insights from Ladson-Billings (2011) and Goff et al. (2014), it is evident that sometime before the age of 10, Black boys are no longer viewed as children. Goff et al. explained the implications of this: When a child is viewed as a child, they are afforded some important protections. In other words, there are qualities and benefits associated with being a child. These include having the ability to make mistakes, being viewed as innocent, being afforded the privilege of protection, and being viewed as needing to be nurtured. Imagine a childhood where these benefits are restricted from one group of children, simply because of the color of their skin. When a group is dehumanized, they no longer have access to the safety and protection necessary for children to grow and thrive.

Aggressive Policing

Aggressive policing is another area that demonstrates the connection and shared patterns between the policing and schooling of Black males. Aggressive policing refers to policies and practices that are overly forceful and punitive. As noted by Ladson-Billings (2011), educators fear Black males, and as a result, educators have a desire to control their actions and movements in ways that are not evident with other populations. This notion of a desire to control is evident in the ways Black lives and minds are engaged in social settings. Table 2 presents the four ways that Black boys and young men are subjected to aggressive policing, this includes excessive engagement, order-maintenance policing, mandatory minimums, and more stringent punishments..

Table 2

Aggressive Policing

Concept	Policing	Schooling
Excessive Engagement	Excessive Use of Force	Violent Handling
Order-Maintenance Policing	Broken Window Policing	Zero Tolerance Policies
Mandatory Minimums	Mandatory Minimum Sentencing	Mandatory Minimum Suspensions and Expulsions
More Stringent Punishments	Lengthier Terms	Lengthier Exclusions

Excessive Engagement

Excessive engagement is one way that aggressive policing is manifested. Excessive engagement refers to the unnecessary and unwarranted handling of Black males. There are many ways that officers can use force in apprehending a suspect. They can push them into walls, throw them to the ground, and draw weapons, among other tactics. In an analysis of the use of force reported by police officers in New York City, Bui and Cox (2016) found that officers are more likely to use force when engaging Blacks. Their research demonstrated that White suspects and Black suspects are engaged in categorically different ways. For example, they found that police officers were 17% more likely to "put hands on" Black suspects than White suspects. Moreover, police officers were more likely to use excessive force on Black suspects by pushing them into walls (by 18%), putting them in handcuffs (by 16%), throwing them to the ground (by 18%), and using pepper spray or batons (by 25%). Even more egregious, officers were 19% more likely to draw weapons and

24% more likely to point those weapons at Black suspects. In fact, Black suspects were overrepresented in every type of use-of-force examined in this analysis.

Other research has examined the use of deadly force with Black suspects. Sadler, Correll, Park, and Judd's (2012) study demonstrated the power of unconscious bias in producing the differential ways that police officers engage Black men. The study consisted of a video game simulation where there were armed and unarmed suspects. The object of the game was to shoot suspects who were armed and to not shoot those who were unarmed. A simple design: Shoot the armed and don't shoot the unarmed. They rotated potential suspects based on racial categories, with potential suspects being Black, White, Latinx, and Asian. Their study examined whether a shot was fired and the time needed to make a decision to "shoot" or "not shoot." Their findings demonstrated the power of the "beasts of prey" view of Black men discussed earlier. They found that Black suspects were more likely to be shot than other suspects. In fact, this occurred when they were armed *and* when they were unarmed. They concluded:

> Racial bias in the amount of time needed to correctly determine whether or not to shoot Blacks perseveres in a multiethnic context. Participants were faster to correctly "shoot" a Black armed target than a White, Latino, or Asian armed target but slower to correctly "not shoot" a Black unarmed target than a White, Latino, or Asian unarmed target. (Sadler et al., 2012, p. 297)

Stated more simplistically, they found that being Black can get you shot.

While the use of force is evident in Black lives, excessive engagement is seen through the violent handling of Black minds in school. Tyrone Howard (2016) has written about this pattern more clearly. He decried the pervasive "violent handling" of Black students, particularly in urban school settings, and he argued that "some might claim that Black students are unfairly targeted in schools by school officers in ways that contribute to the start and sustaining of the criminalizing of students" (Howard, 2016, p. 103). Given the proliferation of school police officers and pseudo-officers in America's schools, it should not be surprising that the treatment of Black males by these officers mirrors what is seen throughout society. There are numerous examples of this, including incidents at Woodland Hills, Rock Round, Tolman, and Northwestern:

- At Woodland Hills School District, Steve Shaulis, a school resource officer, was accused of putting Black males in headlocks, body slamming them to the ground, tasing students while they were held down by the principal, and even knocking out the front teeth of a special needs child (see Judge, 2017).
- At Rock Round High School, Officer Rigo Valles grabbed a Black male by the neck, forced him to the ground, and handcuffed him in front of his peers (see Hanson, 2015).
- At Tolman High School, school resource officer, Jared Boudreault, grabbed a Black male around the throat and body slammed him. The incident resulted in hundreds of students protesting and the subsequent arrest of protesters at that campus (see Crockett, 2015).

- At Northwestern University, a team of officers arrested a Ph.D. student for stealing a car *that he owned*. The student was rushed, kneed, tackled, and punched by officers. After being arrested, one officer told him, "I didn't shoot you . . . you should feel lucky about that" (Boroff, 2017, para. 1).

The cases are but a sample of what has occurred nationally, and these instances are only known because of the power of social media to help hold school officers accountable—at least when the cameras are on. All of these cases have a similar story: The student was not aggressive, did not pose a threat, and the officer escalated the event. Yes, even officers are influenced by the "principal effect."

Order-Maintenance Policing

There is a philosophy in policing referred to as *order-maintenance policing*. Order maintenance policing involves the ways that the use of public space is regulated. Police are empowered to use their authority to regulate public spaces, a role that has been central to police work in the modern era. However, concerns have been raised about the abuse of power in how order is maintained, whose use of space is regulated, and the policies that undergird the use of public space (Thacher, 2014). Broken windows policing (also referred to as quality of life policing and blue summonses) is a primary method of order-maintenance policing. Broken windows policing is informed by the perspective that, if society lets the small crimes go unchecked, then more egregious crimes will occur. Thus, the philosophy is to police the small to prevent the larger issues from occurring. For example, if someone is seen selling loosie (single) cigarettes, riding a bike on the sidewalk, or jaywalking, then they need to receive a citation.

The sensemaking is that if society allows these things to occur, then behavior will spiral out of control. This philosophy has led to many of the challenges facing communities of color. The idea of broken windows policing emanates from the writings of Wilson and Kelling (1982) who discussed their observations on crime. They stated:

> If a window in a building is broken and is left unrepaired, all the rest of the windows will soon be broken. This is as true in nice neighborhoods as in run-down ones . . . one unrepaired broken window is a signal that no one cares. (Wilson & Kelling, 1982, p. 3)

Based on this perspective, broken windows policing is designed to create order by setting normative expectations of behavior through signals—signals that demonstrate that the rule of law is in place, that order is valued, and that even the small issues will be addressed because, according to Wilson and Kelling (1982), "street crime flourishes in neighborhoods in which disorderly behavior goes unchecked" (p. 5).

Broken windows policing is an ineffective policy because it allows for certain communities to be targeted, thereby creating negative police-community relations. For example, a report released by the ACLU (2015) demonstrated the negative outgrowth of broken windows policing in Minneapolis. In an analysis of low-level arrest over a 2.5-year period, they found that Black people were 8.7 times more likely to be arrested for low-level crimes than their White counterparts. These crimes included trespassing, consuming alcohol, disorderly conduct, and "lurking." For instance, Blacks represented only 19% of the population in Minneapolis but accounted for 59%

of arrests for low-level crimes. In comparison, Whites accounted for 64% of the population but only 23% of arrests for low-level crimes.

While Black lives are affected by order maintenance through broken windows policing, Black minds are similarly exposed to these policies under the guise of zero tolerance policies. While zero tolerance has fallen out of favor in large districts, the policy is still in place in many districts across the nation. Zero tolerance policies bring order-maintenance policing to school contexts. Remember, the philosophy is that small issues left unchecked will produce larger issues. So, in school settings, the approach is to discipline every infraction that occurs, no matter how large or small. Zero tolerance policies are designed to create order through the uniform application of consequences for predetermined actions. The goal is to prevent larger infractions from occurring by have "zero" leeway on smaller infractions; otherwise, it is believed that poor behavior will permeate schools where disorder goes unchecked (Curran, 2017). The American Psychological Association (APA) released a report in 2008 from their Zero Tolerance Task Force that was highly critical of zero tolerance policies, noting that it is an erroneous assumption that zero tolerance will improve student disciplinary issues and behavior.

Mandatory Minimums

Black people are subject to mandatory punishments or mandatory minimums more readily than their counterparts. Mandatory minimums require automatic time served for specific infractions, regardless of any contextual factors that may influence the case. They are present in both the policing and schooling of Black males. Mandatory minimums require judges to levy specific penalties based on sentencing guidelines.

According to data from the U.S. Sentencing Commission (2011), Black defendants are more subject to mandatory minimums than their White counterparts. Their analysis included an analysis of sentencing information from nearly 73,000 federal cases. They found that White defendants accounted for 27.4% of the defendant pool. Across sentencing categories, their representation remains constant. For instance, they account for 27.4% of those convicted of a crime with mandatory minimums and 27.5% of those who were subject to a mandatory minimum at sentencing. These data demonstrate equity, in that Whites account for 27% of the population and approximately 27% across all sentencing areas. In contrast, Black defendants account for 20.7% of all offenders. They are grossly overrepresented, accounting for 31.5% of those who were convicted of a crime with a mandatory minimum and 38.5% of those who were subject to a mandatory minimum at sentencing.

To put these data into context, there were only 0.1% more Whites who were convicted of a crime with a mandatory minimum compared to their population in the defender pool. In contrast, there was a 17.8% higher representation among Blacks defendants in this same designation. Mandatory minimums are often made worse by sentencing enhancements. Sentencing enhancements allow (and sometimes require) judges to provide an added penalty of time for certain aggravating factors, such as the defendants criminal history, weapons charges, and gang affiliation. These enhancements often extend mandatory minimums in a way that adversely affects Black men. According to the ACLU (2014b):

> Scholars have also noted that federal . . . sentencing
> enhancements, which at a minimum double a federal drug

defendant's mandatory minimum sentence and may raise the maximum sentence from 40 years to life without parole, if the defendant has two prior qualifying drug convictions in state or federal courts, are applied by federal prosecutors in an arbitrary and racially discriminatory manner and exacerbate racial disparities in the criminal justice system. (p. 14)

While mandatory minimums adversely affect Black lives in policing, they also directly influence Black minds in schools. In school settings, the equivalent practice is the use of mandatory minimum suspensions and expulsions for certain infractions. Just as with mandatory minimum sentencing, mandatory suspensions and expulsions can be applied arbitrarily based on the perceived infraction. Here too, the evidence of conscious and unconscious bias is evident in our social systems. For example, in some Texas districts, an assault would trigger a mandatory minimum suspension, whereas a fight would not necessarily do so (though it would prompt some type of action). However, what constitutes the difference between an assault versus a fight can be subject to the perception of the educators who see and write up the infractions. For example, in a brief analysis of mandatory minimum policies, I found that a fight viewed as mutual combat often triggers a 2-day out-of-school suspension, but an assault often prompts a 3-day or more out-of-school suspension, contact with law enforcement, and additional probationary factors for the student upon their return. The following represents language that might be seen in a mandatory minimums policy:

- "A student who has committed a violent act will be subject to a 5-day or more suspension."

- "A student who has been substantially disruptive of the learning environment will be subject to a 5-day or more suspension."
- "A student who hinders the authority of an educator will be subject to a 5-day or more suspension."

This language was informed by policies identified in the state of Rhode Island. The inherent distrust of Black males through the lens of overcriminalization produces circumstances where the view of what has occurred may vary across racial/ethnic groups. This is evidenced by data from the U.S. Office of Civil Rights (2014b) that found young Black men were overrepresented among those exposed to expulsions.

More Stringent Punishments

Beyond being subject to mandatory minimums, Black defendants also receive more stringent punishments. These punishments are evidenced via lengthier terms. This encompasses lengthier terms in sentencing and in suspensions and expulsions. With respect to Black lives, individuals can be exposed to lengthier terms in two ways. The first is time served for those who are found innocent of the crimes of which they are accused. A report from the U.S. Department of Justice on detentions in New York County provides evidence that Black defendants are more likely to go to jail after arraignment for a misdemeanor. The report found that 88% of White defendants were released on their own recognizance compared to 76% of Black defendants. After being arraigned, only 10% of White defendants went to jail compared to 22% of Black defendants. In terms of felony crimes, a higher rate of post-detention jailing occurs, though this rate is still higher for Black defendants.

For example, 41% of White defendants will be held in jail, while 59% of Black defendants will be. These data may demonstrate that Black defendants will spend more time in jail, even for crimes they may not be convicted of in the future (Kutateladze & Andiloro, 2014). While a person may receive time served if convicted, an individual who is not found guilty or found guilty of a lesser crime would have served time anyhow. Kahn and Kirk's (2015) study indicated:

> blacks were more likely than whites or nonblack minorities to be in jail while they await trial, even after controlling for the seriousness of charges and prior record . . . this disparity is often due to the fact that black defendants cannot afford to pay bail. The temporary incarceration stigmatizes the defendant, disrupts family life and employment, and makes it harder for the defendant to prepare a defense. (para. 4)

The second way that an individual can be exposed to a lengthier term is at sentencing. In 2016, the Editorial Board at *The New York Times* did an exposé on sentencing bias called "Same Crime, More Time." Their efforts focused on the State of Florida and highlighted a county in the state called Flagler. In this county, Black defendants convicted of robbery were sentenced to nearly 7 years, this is three times the rate of Whites convicted of the same crime with similar circumstances. When taking into account felony drug possession, Black defendants were sentenced to 107% more days in prison than their White counterparts. However, the most egregious difference was in Okeechobee County where Blacks spent 179% more time in prison than Whites. Their exposé concluded by noting that "Blacks were given much longer prison sentences in Florida than Whites for felony drug possession involving the same circumstances" (para. 7).

While more stringent punishments result in lengthier sentences, stringent punishments in school settings result in lengthier exclusions from the classroom. Kinsler (2011) conducted an analysis of 500,000 student records from 1,000 public schools located in North Carolina. In this study, the examination focused on disparities between the extensiveness and intensiveness of the punishment. Extensiveness refers to the pervasiveness of those punished as measured via the overall percentage. Intensiveness refers to the length of the punishment levied, as assessed by the total number of days. This research demonstrated that Black students received greater punishments for the same infractions, both in terms of extensiveness and intensiveness. Black students received significantly more suspensions for discipline referrals, rule violations, undisciplined behavior, and aggressive behavior in elementary school and middle school. Moreover, they received longer suspensions across all categories as well. In all, they were suspended more often and for longer periods of time. The analysis also focused on the race of the teachers and principals who were rendering these suspensions. Interestingly, they found that there was no difference in the suspensions levied by race, meaning that a Black principal was just as likely to suspend a Black child as a White principal. This point speaks to the insidiousness of unconscious and conscious bias in our society.

Racial Profiling

Racial profiling is another area where comparisons can be easily drawn between the policing of Black lives and the schooling of Black minds. This is evidenced through racial profiling at the community level (i.e., community targeting) and the personal level (i.e., individual targeting). Racial profiling occurs when a group of people are "targeted," surveilled, and engaged by police officers at greater rates simply due to their racial/ethnic heritage. Black communities have a long and adverse relationship with police officers due to profiling practices that constantly "mark" Black people as criminalized.

Table 3

Racial Profiling

Concept	Policing	Schooling
Community Targeting	Hot-Spot Policing	Hot-Spot Schooling
Individual Targeting	Stop and Frisk Driving While Black	Schooling While Black

Community Targeting

In policing, there is a practice of identifying areas for enhanced intervention using an approach called hot-spot policing. In hot-spot policing, maps of crimes for a specific region are examined. These maps are examined to identify areas where there is a high density of crime occurring. The logic of this approach is that policing these areas of dense crime (i.e., hot spots) can serve to reduce overall crime. This tactic has been used by many law enforcement leaders as a strategy for raising their visibility and reputation (Dunham & Alpert, 2015). They identify crime hot spots, concentrate resources and highly police those areas, and then use this to show that they have reduced overall crime. Sanchez and Rosenbaum (2011) have critiqued this practice:

> Police organizations that measure performance by the numbers (e.g., arrests, gun seizures, drugs, money) and

that deploy large numbers of police officers to minority communities to combat "hot spots" of crime, could be accused of "racially profiling communities" (rather than individuals) and contributing to disproportionate minority mistreatment, arrests, and confinement. (p. 174)

The logic behind this approach must be weighed against the fact that the practice is mostly used in urban settings and "there is no set standard for identifying and defining crime hot spots" (National Institute of Justice, 2005, para. 2). This lack of clarity on how to determine what does and does not constitute a hot spot produces a circumstance where unconscious and conscious bias can influence decision-making. Moreover, the limited availability of resources can further influence the decision-making process. The challenge produced by community targeting is that it can further foster negative police-community relations, as community members believe (accurately) that their communities are being profiled.

Community targeting occurs through hot-spot policing, but also manifests through hot-spot schooling. Hot-spot schooling refers to the concentration of school resource officers, private security, and police officers in schools. As noted by Howard (2016), there is a high presence of these "policing" agents in low-income schools and schools with high percentages of students of color. While this pattern is true for low-income schools, it is even more concerning at predominantly minority-serving schools. For example, 41.6% of affluent-serving schools (defined as having 25% or less of their students on free and reduced lunch) had security staff present. In contrast, 45.8% of low-income serving schools (defined as having 75% or more of their students on free and reduced lunch) had security staff (Digest of Education, 2015). However, this difference between schools with high percentages of students of color are even more visible.

According to the Digest of Education Statistics (2015), 35.6% of schools that are predominantly White (defined as having less than 5% students of color) have security staff compared to 48% of schools that are predominantly minority-serving (defined as having 50% or more students of color). These data demonstrate that minority-serving schools are being targeted as "hot spots" for in-school policing. These data only account for security staff and do not demonstrate the further disparities evident through the policing done by police officers who are not on staff at the school.

Individual Targeting

While racial profiling can occur at a community level, it can also take place at the individual level regardless of whether the individual resides or does not reside in a "minority" community. One example of this is the "Stop and Frisk" or "Stop – Question and Frisk" policy evident in a number of large cities. "Stop and Frisk" is used to identify criminals by stopping, detaining, questioning, and searching suspects for weapons or guns. The policy has been infamously employed in New York and came under intense scrutiny following a report released by the New York Civil Liberties Union in 2011. In their report, they found that Blacks and Latinos accounted for 87% of all individuals who were subjected to the Stop and Frisk policy. In comparison, only 13% of non-Black and non-Latino individuals were stopped using this policy.

While this policy was a known and enacted written policy, an informal practice that also continues to profile Black peoples is

"Driving While Black" (DWB). DWB refers to Black people being targeted and pulled over in vehicles based on the color of their skin. The vast majority of African Americans have, at one point of another, been targeted for DWB. The Bureau of Justice Statistics (2011), which assesses contact between community members and police, found that there was evidence of racial profiling. The Bureau found that African American were 31% more likely to be pulled over by police officers despite having no infractions or for small infractions. This included minor issues such as having a broken light, failure to signal, or rolling through stop. Interestingly, these are data that are reported by police officers themselves and are likely underreported.

Being targeted for DWB is a practice that has resulted in the unjustified imprisonment and death of African Americans. For example, the Philando Castile case represents an example of this. According to Mannix (2016), the police officer in the Castile case "decided the car looked suspicious. He radioed to a nearby squad that he was going to pull it over and check IDs of the driver and passenger." The officer stated, "The two occupants just look like people that were involved in a robbery . . . the driver looks more like one of our suspects, just because of the wide-set nose. I couldn't get a good look at the passenger." As you may know, Castile was pulled over with his girlfriend and baby in the car. The officer approached the car and informed Castile that he was being pulled over for a broken brake light. Castile stated, "Sir, I have to tell you, I do have a firearm." The officer said, "Don't pull it out." Castile indicated multiple times that he was not pulling out the gun or reaching for it before being fired upon and killed inside the car. Even after being shot multiple times, Castile exclaimed that he was not reaching for the gun.

In schools, the same pattern that took the life of Philando Castile occurs as well. Black children are subject to "Schooling While Black," being singled-out for innocuous actions. For example, a study conducted by Gilliam and colleagues (2016) used video clips to examine the differential ways that teachers in preschool tracked students' behavior. The teachers were told they would be viewing video clips of children engaging in poor behaviors, and they were told they needed to identify the poor behavior as it was unfolding. In reality, none of the clips actually showed bad behaviors. However, the real focus of the study was to track the eye movements of the teachers to determine if there was a difference in who they monitored when looking for "bad" behaviors. Their findings indicated that preschool teachers spent more time looking for disruptive behaviors in Black children than in White children. In other words, when primed to look for potentially bad behavior among preschoolers, the object of focus was Black children.

The pattern of being "singled out" is evident early on in students' educational experiences. For instance, it is not uncommon to find that two boys who are playing on the schoolyard are engaged differently by educators. Both may be engaged in some form of "rough" play, but one can be singled out for discipline while the other is lauded for the same actions, the only difference between the two being their racial/ethnic background. More often than not, the pattern is that Black boys are disciplined for innocuous rough play while their White male peers are not (Howard, 2013b; Wood & Harris III,

2017)—two children facing two very different experiences in the same classroom or schoolyard.

In 2016, Frank Harris III and I wrote about "Schooling While Black" in an article we wrote in the *Huffington Post*. The article was titled, "Too Smart to Succeed, Too Good to Win." In the article, we talked about what occurs when men of color outperform low expectations. This article, based on our research on Black men in community colleges, found that high performing men of color can be targeted for being "too good" and "too smart." Here is one quote that helps to contextualize this pattern:

> English has always been my favorite subject and I've always really enjoyed writing. In my English comp class, we had to write a 10-page essay on a social issue. I wrote mine on police brutality and the professor accused me of plagiarism! When he was handing back the papers, there was a note on mine that said, "Please come and see me in my office." There was no grade on the paper, so I figured something was up. When I went to see him, he asked me, "Who wrote this paper?" I told him I did. He said he didn't believe me . . . I told him I always enjoyed writing and was really good at it. He said he still didn't believe me, but since he didn't have proof that I cheated, he would "let me go" this time but I better be careful.

In the data we have collected, we found the pattern described in this quote to be pervasive. In these cases, Black men write strong papers and score well on tests and exams, but because there are low expectations for their performance, they are accused of cheating rather than being lauded for their performance and efforts. As demonstrated in this chapter, there are a number of ways that the policing of Black lives and schooling of Black minds are similar. These patterns help to demonstrate why the schools are so effective in socializing Black males for prison and why, for many Black males, school is a prison. In the next chapter, I extend Black Minds Pedagogy as a strategy for educators who seek to foster new, more productive realities for our Black boys and men in education.

Personal Story – Nameless Names

In February of 1982, I entered into the world—a mere 3 minutes after my twin brother. At the time, our biological mother, Joann, was in prison, but she had been brought to the hospital for our delivery. Joann was a brilliant woman; in fact, she had always been academically gifted. She had studied psychology at several prestigious institutions, served as a part-time professor at a university in San Francisco, and was said to possess a doctorate (Ph.D.) in the same field. Despite these accomplishments, she struggled mightily with mental health issues. She had always been eccentric from an early age, but significant familial losses, persistent stress, and substance abuse served as a toxic combination that propelled a downward spiral. These factors, combined with a tumultuous relationship with her ex-husband, led to her imprisonment, which may have been our saving grace. She was in prison for a large part of her pregnancy, reducing the timeframe of our exposure to illicit substances.

She gave my brother and I angel names, Gabriel and Ariel—powerful names to protect us as we moved forward into a life that she would never engage. In reality, Joann had no capacity to raise us, nor the desire to do so. In fact, she had, at times, sought to relieve herself of our burden near the later stages of her pregnancy. In her desperation to end the pregnancy, she would run from one end of her cell to the other, banging her stomach against the bars. She did so repeatedly until she was stopped. As a result, she spent a significant part of the end of her pregnancy in restraints and in a padded cell to prevent further prenatal trauma. Soon after our births, Joann returned to prison, and my brother and I became wards of the court. We were immediately placed into the foster care system. Three days after our birth, we were given to a foster family as a temporary placement. Joann's names for us were never shared with the family and never made it onto our birth certificates. The foster family was told that my brother was Baby A and I was Baby B—even our birth certificates read the same. Nameless names.

In the car on the way to their home, we were given the names Joshua and Luke, biblical names emblematic of our adoptive mother's strong Christian faith. Due to Joann's illicit drug use, her very poor mental health, and the prenatal trauma we experienced, there was much concern about the prospect of our future. Our foster mother, Karen, and her eldest daughter prayed over us daily, hoping that prayer would protect us from what may have seemed an inevitably challenging future. For months, we remained with the same family as a temporary placement. Our first crawls, first steps, and first words were shared without Joann and instead with the family who covered us in prayer. Two years after our birth, Joann had exited prison and was revolving back and forth from homelessness to government housing. All the while, the social worker who oversaw our case tried to track her down and find out what her plans for us were. Once she finally got in touch with Joann, she provided her with a pathway to restore custody. Joann agreed to a series of meetings with us.

The meetings were set with the greatest of caution, with plans for her to enter into the front door of the foster agency, while our foster parents entered privately through the back door. The first meeting was set, and she was unable to make it. Other attempts met a similar outcome—she scheduled but never came. It is possible that she wanted to but could not. Maybe her transportation failed, or maybe she was terrified to travel due to her mental health. I have often thought of the various rationales that would lead her to no-show time and time again. These rationales have, at times, provided a sense of solace in the face of an unmistakable truth: We were not wanted, at least not enough for her to come.

Regardless of the potential rationales, she never came to see the twin boys she had carried in her womb and birthed into the world. Then, communication with Joann went dark—she was nowhere to be found. The social worker tried arduously to locate her, but she was difficult to find. She shifted continuously between homes, hotels, and less desirable living options. One day, the social worker was finally able to track her down, and it was that day that she gave my brother and me the greatest gift she could ever give. She released us. I am not sure how the conversation transpired, but I know that she was asked whether she wanted to pursue restoring custody, and I know she said, "I don't want to ever see them again." Upon hearing these words as an adult, I was immediately pained. They reveal a disposition that I cannot fully understand. I cannot imagine the emotional distress that she must have been under to relinquish her rights to have us. I have tried to imagine that her harsh words were uttered with restricted emotionality that soon faded behind a sea of sharp tears after the social worker departed. I will never know, and maybe it is best that I do not. Ultimately, Joann gave my brother and me a precious gift— the chance at a better life that she knew she was unable to provide.

After she relinquished her rights, the foster agency moved forward to establish a permanent placement. Upon hearing the news, our foster family was informed that they should be prepared for us to transition out of the home as a more "suitable" family had been identified to adopt us. The concern of suitability arose from the fact that our foster parents were White and we are African American. While transracial adoptions had been more common in prior decades, such placements had become increasingly taboo by the early 1980s. The agency had identified a Black family they felt would be a better fit for raising us in a society defined by race, racism, and asymmetries of power.

Our foster mother was devastated. The news struck her like a punch to the stomach; she felt sick and overwhelmed. Karen promptly called John, our case worker's supervisor, and informed him that we were "her children," and that she believed "God had given us to her." He informed her that the decision had already been made and to prepare for the transition. To this, she responded, "Please do me a favor. If you still plan to move them, let me know. At least allow me the opportunity to hire an attorney." Angrily, John hung up the phone. One month went by, then two—still no word. Then, Karen attended a foster parent meeting about another child who needed placement, and to her surprise, the social worker congratulated Karen on receiving approval to adopt us. She was noticeably shocked and overjoyed. The social worker said, "No one told you, John never called you?" Karen replied, "It doesn't matter, thank you." The social worker informed Karen that she and several other social workers in the agency had approached John with a list of pros as to why she should be approved to adopt us. They said, "We think you are making a mistake here. If you can come up with as many cons as we have pros, then we will support you." Apparently, his list was not as long.

Nearly three years after we entered into the foster care system, we were adopted by the same family that had taken us home, prayed over us, and raised us since birth. No longer nameless names, we were Joshua Wood and Luke Wood. Our parents were veteran foster parents, and by the time of our adoption, they already had three children of their own, two foster children under permanent legal guardianship (one wheelchair bound and the other with a mental disability), two adopted children (my twin brother and me), and several other foster children in the home. Needless to say, our home was large. Moreover, many of us were of different ethnic backgrounds—White, Black, Latino, Hawaiian, and more. We were a collection of throwaways, the children whose parents had abandoned them in dumpsters, brutalized them with fire, shot them up with drugs, and disregarded them. But we were one family, multiracial and multifaceted.

CHAPTER 3

BLACK MINDS PEDAGOGY

How can you prepare a teacher to go to teach in a place that you have never been?. . . Many faculty who are in teacher education have not taught in an urban school, have never experienced Black male students in an academic setting, have never experienced their culture, have never experienced the realities of dealing with their communities...and now this person is charged with preparing somebody else to go into this setting.

– Chance Lewis, Distinguished Professor,
University of North Carolina at Charlotte
(Statement from Black Minds Matter)

Over the years, I have enjoyed the honor and privilege of serving as a trainer for "diversity" issues at many schools, colleges, and universities throughout the nation. Alongside my colleague Frank Harris III, I have enjoyed opportunities to engage in meaningful conversations with thousands of educators across numerous states, institutional types, and political climates. Much of our training has focused on teaching practices for boys and men of color and intensive trainings on racial microaggressions and unconscious bias in education. Racial microaggressions and unconscious bias are two concepts that tend to meld well together, as unconscious bias (unknown racist tendencies) are often manifested most clearly through microaggressions (unconscious racial slights directed toward people of color).

As part of our training, we ask educators to engage in an exercise where they describe some of their earliest experiences with Black boys and men. In particular, we are interested in experiences that occurred when they were children or youth that resonate with them. These can be images they saw on television, comments heard from friends and family, initial interactions with members from these groups, or depictions in physical or virtual media. We probe them to tell us about the most formative experiences that come to mind when they hear the terms "Black boys" or "Black men." Their comments include positive images, but most commonly elucidate negative depictions, images, and representations of Black males.

The comments always provide insights into why the negative stereotypes of Black men are so widely engrained in our society. They also show the enduring power of the media and our families in shaping our views of Black people, particularly Black boys and men. Most commonly, the remarks from my colleagues fall into four recurrent categories. First, they include television programming that featured Black characters, families, and talent in a comedic light. This commonly includes *Sanford and Son, Good Times, Diff'rent Strokes, Fat Albert, A Different World, Fresh Prince of Bel Air, Amos 'n' Andy*, and almost invariably, *The Cosby Show*. Particularly among White audiences, we find that their earliest exposure to Black people was not through personal interactions, but shaped through popular television shows and characters. Though often heartwarming, these shows are not accurate representations of the diversity of Black life and culture, but are sitcoms designed for enjoyment. They leverage stereotypes of Black people as jokesters and buffoons (Bogle, 2001). These shows have introduced and socialized popular conceptions of Black people to adoring White audiences. Early images of Black men as comedians are another aspect of this. Individuals often invoke the names of famed comedians such as Sammie Davis Jr., Richard Pryor, Martin Lawrence, Redd Foxx, Eddie Murphy, Chris Rock, and Dick Gregory. These individuals are talked about with reverence for their talent, artistic poise, and ability to turn a phrase. These names further reinforce the pervasive presentation of Black men as having comedic talent.

Another popular description of Black men included early exposure to Black musicians. You will also hear participants utter the names of musical artists, such as Michael Jackson and Prince. For Michael Jackson, you often hear callouts to his original group, The Jackson Five, and to his nickname, The King of Pop. Others will say the names of some of his most popular songs, such as "Smooth Criminal," "Thriller," and "Black or White." For Prince, the most common call-out beyond references to his name (e.g., Prince, the Artist formerly known as Prince) are references to "Purple Rain." The words are often called out publicly with glee, adjoining these names as artifacts that testify to their greatness. Younger audiences refer to artists such as Drake, Jay-Z, and Kanye West.

A popular third description is of Black males as athletes. This can include seeing young Black males playing sports like football and basketball. Even more frequently, responses highlight the "best of the best" of Black athletes. Names such as Wilt "the Stilt" Chamberlain, Michael Jordan, Lebron James, and Kobe Bryant are spoken about with reverence for their contributions to their respective sports. However, the most common response in this category is "The Juice," O.J. Simpson. As an athlete, O.J. placed an indelible impact on the formative experiences of a generation who lauded him for his athletic prowess and ability to ingratiate himself to White audiences. Unfortunately, O.J. also has the unique distinction of residing in this category while also falling into the next category as well.

The fourth category is early images of Black men as criminals. People often encapsulate their experiences with single words and catchphrases that extol Black hypercriminality, including "gangsters," "criminals," "dangerous," "pusher," "pimps," and "drug dealers." Participants also regularly describe growing up listening to the radio or watching the nightly news and seeing Black men who were wanted for horrendous crimes. When asked to further describe these news flashes, the crowd will remember depictions of Black men as "rapists," "murderers," "armed and dangerous," and "violent." As noted, O.J. Simpson and the "Trial of the Century" is likely the most recurrent theme in this category. Whenever the trial is mentioned—the White Bronco, the gloves, or key individuals, such as Johnny Cochrane, Robert Shapiro, and Marcia Clark—the demeanor of the crowd often becomes immediately and palpably polarized.

Lastly, colleagues have also shared the negative perceptions of Black neighborhoods, life, and culture. This theme tends to intersect with other themes, particularly around images of Black criminality. Some will talk about individuals being poorly dressed, destitute, and "needing help." Colleagues have also shared about being in the car with parents or grandparents who pointed to the "other side of tracks" (i.e., communities with high concentrations of Black individuals) and remarked that they should avoid these areas, not go into them at night, and lock their doors and roll up their windows (even when driving). They were told early on by people they loved that these neighborhoods were "bad," "dangerous," or "run down." They also describe similarly disparaging comments about the people who live in these areas as having unstructured homes, not having good values, being fatherless, and the like. Many will refer to riots, particularly the Los Angeles Riots and the Detroit Riots (during the "Long Hot Summer"), as being salient early images engrained in their minds. Overall, these descriptions paint a negative picture of Black life and culture as being "lesser than."

These five themes demonstrate that the earliest images of Black men are as comedians, musicians, athletes (e.g., particularly basketball and football players), criminals, and include negative perceptions of Black neighborhoods, life, and culture. These early depictions matter because of a concept called *the primacy effect*. The primacy effect refers to the fact that individuals tend to give more weight to information presented earlier when forming opinions and making decisions. Thus, the earliest experiences shape how we view information presented later (Noguchi, Kamada, & Shrira, 2014). This concept can be applied in a number of ways. For example, in argumentation, it is often said that the first person to make an argument has the strongest argument. This is because every argument that comes afterwards is shaped as a response to that argument—it is a counterargument.

This occurs in socialization as well. The early experiences we have as children tend to shape how we view and interpret information as adults. Thus, the most formative memories of Black boys and men shape how they are viewed. Given that many schools, communities, and religious institutions remain segregated, this suggests that the most predominant viewpoints of Black males are shaped, not by interactions with them, but through the media. These depictions almost invariably paint Black males as amusing and athletic, yet lowly, unintelligent, and criminalized.

Unfortunately, early experiences with Black males emanate from a society rife with stereotypes. The primacy effect suggests that these influence us greatly. Moreover, research has shown that the formative experiences we have that are bad or negative are more powerful than those that are good. Not surprisingly, the bad messages we hear, images we see, and experiences we have tend to shape us more readily than the good ones. Thus, while the primacy effect is shaped by good early images, bad early images tend to carry more weight (Baumeister, Bratslavsky, Finkenauer, & Vohs, 2001). Being loveable is second to being unintelligent, and being entertaining is second to being a criminal.

These patterns tend to translate three key messages that are the focus of Black Minds Pedagogy. As aligned with prior inquiry (Fain, 2015), these three key messages are seen in the ways educators engage Black males in educational institutions. First, the depictions of Black men in sitcoms and as comedians, athletes, and even musicians, to some extent, are largely constructed in ways that highlight specific talents, while deemphasizing academic talents. While endearing, these images further propel wider viewpoints that Black men are unintelligent. This has perpetuated stereotypes about Black academic inferiority. Second, the pervasive depictions of Black men as criminals translate to educators engaging them through criminalized viewpoints. As such, they are engaged with a sense of fear, a desire to control, and in overly aggressive manners. Third, the insidious depictions of Black neighborhoods, life, and culture often communicate a pathologized view of Black people. This results in Black people being engaged as abhorrent and lesser than.

The D-Three Effect

In an article published by the *Journal of African American Males in Education,* my colleagues and I recounted the three primary ways that Black boys and men are viewed, and subsequently engaged, in educational settings (see Wood, Blevins, & Essien, 2017). Largely, these patterns emerged from collaborative research on men of color in community colleges (Wood & Harris III, 2017), but are certainly emblematic of their larger educational experiences from preschool to doctoral education. We refer to these patterns as the D-three effect, or the tendency of educators to advance deficit narratives of Black boys and men that communicate Distrust, Disdain, and Disregard. This occurs both overtly and covertly. Moreover, these experiences align with three of the microaggression subtypes espoused by Derald Wing Sue (Sue et al., 2007). Microaggressions refer to subtle actions that degrade, insult, and invalidate people of color. They can be both verbal and nonverbal in nature and are often rendered unconsciously from one individual to another. While the D-three are inclusive of these unconscious renderings, they are also inclusive of direct and overt messages and actions that communicate racial indignations to Black males.

The first way that Black boys and men are viewed is through a lens of Distrust. Through this lens, research affirms that Black boys and men are viewed in a criminalized manner, perceived as deviant, nefarious, troublemakers, and having malintent (Noguera, 2003). The second lens that Black males are viewed through is Disdain. This entails the ways this population is pathologized. Specifically, this refers to deficit perspectives of students, their families, and their communities (Harper, 2009), including frequent portrayals as being "lazy," "uncaring," or the root cause of disparate outcomes in educational settings. One common example that my colleague Frank Harris III and I have found in our work in community colleges is that some faculty will frame Black males as being in college for ulterior motives, stating, "They are not really here for school, they are just here for the financial aid." This message is among many negative perspectives that educators often hold about Black males (Wood & Harris III, 2017b). The third pattern is Disregard, which includes dismissing (or disregarding) the intelligence of this population or their worth in terms of their ability to perform academically and to positively contribute to the learning environment. Throughout the educational experience of Black boys and men, the D-three effect is in place. This tendency is manifested by school teachers, counselors, administrators, and sometimes even parents.

Black Minds Pedagogy

The D-three effect is powerful and all-encompassing in the schooling of Black minds. In response, Black Minds Pedagogy is a principle of practice that aggressively and unapologetically countermessages the dominant deficit narratives about Black boys and men. Therefore, a Black Minds Pedagogy intentionally extolls the brilliance, dignity, and morality of Black minds. Brilliance, dignity, and morality serve to counterbalance disregard, disdain, and distrust, respectively. These affirmations should be noticeably present in relational dynamics, built environments, teaching and learning, and classroom artifacts. They should be evident in every aspect of the formal and informal schooling of Black boys and men.

To be proactive in extending these affirmations is to be antiracist. To not engage this principle of practice is racist—for to not build up those who are constantly being drawn down is to participate in their destruction. This requires educators to bear an asset-based perspective on Black lives and minds, consciously rejecting deficit perspectives.

Slavers Row Your Boat Ashore

Intentional thinking, discussion, and action that extols Black minds is meant to counter the D-three effect. As such, Black Minds Pedagogy is an act of civil resistance. This principle of practice is important because it takes the notion of racial justice in education beyond its normal resting place. Consider this, a group of men are in a rowboat with their oars in the water. They are all rowing in the same direction. This boat represents the systemic racism facing our Black boys and men. At some point, one man becomes aware that, by rowing, he is being complicit in fostering injustice. Aware of this fact, he lifts his oars out of the water to stop contributing to the movement of the boat. As an educator, this is the equivalent of being cautious to avoid conveying bias, microaggressions, and working to build a more "fair" educational environment. Unfortunately, this is an action far too many educators take, even those who consider themselves to be relatively conscious. They believe that, by not contributing to the pervasive distrust, disdain, and disregard of Black males, they are doing the right thing. Certainly, the act of removing themselves from doing so is important, but it does nothing to stop the direction or the momentum of the boat.

In contrast, another rower similarly recognizes that he is complicit in carrying out injustice. As a response, he lifts his oars out of the water and instead of leaving them there, he begins to paddle in the other direction. With all his might, he rows, harder and harder, knowing that his disruption is vital, knowing that his efforts, for many, are a matter of life and death. His actions are akin to extolling the brilliance, dignity, and morality of Black minds in and out of the classroom. This goes beyond withdrawal from racist practices to being purposefully antiracist.

This analogy paints a picture of three types of people in educational settings—those who are slavers, those who are sympathizers of the freedom movement, and those who are abolitionists. Slavers engage, unknowingly and sometimes knowingly, in the destruction of Black males by perpetuating the D-three effect. Sympathizers are intentional about being nonracist themselves, but they fail to engage in practices that can liberate their students or hold their colleagues accountable. Abolitionists are antiracist educators who proactively extol the brilliance, dignity, and morality of Black minds. A civil resistance requires action; therefore, it is not enough to desire another's freedom (as a sympathizer); one must actively seek to abolish the ideologies, practices, and narratives that maintain the system of oppression.

Black Minds Pedagogy as a Form of Antiracist, Culturally Relevant Teaching

Given this, Black Minds Pedagogy is rooted in the scholarly tradition of antiracist pedagogy, with a specific focus on antiracism around issues of distrust, disdain, and disregard. Beyond this, it is also directly connected to culturally relevant teaching. For years, scholars have advanced different conceptualizations of teaching practices that connect the classroom learning experience to the lived sociocultural experiences of students. This notion is embodied in the terms *culturally responsive, culturally compatible, culturally congruent, culturally sensitive*, and *culturally appropriate teaching* (see Ladson-Billings, 1995). These practices recognize that there is often incongruence between the school cultures, languages, and ways of being compared to those in students' homes. This disconnect is seen as a primary inhibitor of students' learning, development, and success. Therefore, these practices espouse the importance of connecting the lived sociocultural experiences of students to classroom instruction. This involves using teaching styles, classroom materials, and concept examples that resonate with students. For instance, Pewewardy (1993) argued that there is a need to go beyond integrating culture into schooling to ultimately integrate schooling into culture. There is a need to engage a "pervasive integration of ideas, images, texts, and experiences that reflect the culture and lives of students" (Wood & Harris III, 2017a, p. 50).

Black Minds Pedagogy is merely one strategy that can aid educators in achieving the desired ends of culturally centered teaching. My conceptualization of this form of pedagogy is rooted in the concept of culturally relevant teaching. According to Ladson-Billings (1995), culturally relevant teaching is a pedagogy of opposition that is committed to collective empowerment. She argued that culturally relevant teaching must expose students to opportunities for success, develop their cultural competence, and foster a crucial consciousness that enables them to confront societal oppression. Thus, culturally relevant teaching goes beyond having content that is relevant to the daily lives and experiences of diverse students; it must also seek to empower them. As noted by Ladson-

Billings, this includes better preparing students to take on the societal challenges and oppression their communities face. Bearing this in mind, Black Minds Pedagogy has two primary goals: first, fostering greater agency in Black students' lives, and second, preparing Black students to confront oppressive societal forces.

There are a number of strategies to facilitate culturally relevant teaching. In fact, in previous works (e.g., Wood & Harris III, 2017a; Wood et al., 2015), I have discussed these strategies: (a) learning about students' backgrounds and experiences and connecting course examples to these realities; (b) allowing students to select readings and assignments; (c) engaging in problem-based learning; and (d) inviting diverse guest speakers to class meetings to speak to students in person or through videoconferencing. There are manifold benefits of a culturally relevant pedagogy. Specifically, Wood and Harris III (2017a) found that culturally relevant teaching "communicates to students that educators value their perspectives and beliefs, makes course material more meaningful and easier to understand, increases student engagement, connects students to class learning, and creates a greater sense of belonging in school" (pp. 49-50). Certainly, these are outcomes that must be fostered for Black males.

Barriers to Culturally Centered Instruction

Two of the most pervasive barriers to the implementation of culturally centered pedagogy is preparation and the availiability of resources to support this type of instruction. Preparation refers to the readiness of educators to engage students through a culturally relevant teaching practice. In postsecondary education, the vast majority of educators are subject matter experts who possess incredible intellectual capacity but have little (if any) training in teaching. For example, in the average community college, a professor of biology has earned a bachelor's degree in biology, holds a master's degree in biology, and worked in industry for a period of time. Few have ever received training on how to teach students. So, in response, educators engage a recurrent paradigm that has plagued education since its inception: They teach how they were taught. Unfortunately, how they were taught is not how our students of color learn.

Without formal training in teaching, their only recourse is to model what they have seen from others using their own student experience as a framework for what to do. The incongruity between these modalities and the learning styles of students is conspicuous. For the few who have training in teaching, their exposure to development opportunities is typically limited in nature and often does not include teaching strategies and practices that are specific to learners of color. Even if they are taught how to teach, they may not be taught how to teach the students who they will actually encounter in their classes.

While K-12 teachers are credentialed (for the most part) and benefit from preservice training programs on teaching, the preparation of K-12 educators to teach diverse student populations is woefully lacking as well. Too few programs place the necessary emphasis on topical areas such as unconscious bias, microaggressions, cultural competency, crosscultural communication, and teaching strategies for diverse learners. These topics are essential for preparing predominantly White teachers to engage and educate students of color. Therefore, the patterns evident in K-12 only worsen when students reach postsecondary education, if they reach it at all.

While preparation is a concern, the resources to engage a culturally centered pedagogy is also inhibited by availability.

Resources include texts, curricula, teaching materials, and classroom resources designed to facilitate the learning of culturally diverse students. Too few textbooks adequately prioritize the diverse historical and contemporary contributions of people of color. Instead, these textbooks only serve to reify the notion that knowledge, technological and medical innovations, and theoretical advancements emanate from White communities. This centers White learners in the classroom and decenters Black learners (and other learners of color), positioning knowledge and an ideology of Whiteness together as one. This exclusion applies to both content coverage (Araújo & Maeso, 2012) and images about Black people in textbooks (Collins & Hebert, 2008).

Even when Blacks are acknowledged in textbooks, they are represented in ways that have been characterized as "reductive," "overly simplistic," and "stereotypical" (see Woodson, 2015). In fact, even educators who are consciously aware of this pattern struggle to find readily available resources that can effectively support culturally centered instruction. I have often been asked by faculty colleagues where to find resources or whether I can recommend resources that would be good to use. The truth is, while there are certainly some resources available, it is often incumbent upon the educator to do more reading and preparation to identify appropriate resources for their specific content. This inevitably takes more time, thereby further exacerbating the problem.

Even in children's books, culturally centered material is scant. As noted by Donna Ford during her appearance on Black Minds Matter, only 3% of children's books are written about African Americans. She noted that the underrepresentation of books that mirror the lives and experiences of students can lead to aliteracy - choosing not to read (Wood, 2018). Moreover, the authenticity of this 3% is questionable, as 76% of children's books about African Americans are written by non-Black authors (Horning, 2017). As a result, there is a need for more books, textbooks, and materials that focus on people of color, are written by people of color, have diverse characters and figures, and have content that connect to themes relevant in students' personal lives (Wood & Harris III, 2017a).

The following three chapters provide more context for what constitutes Black Minds Pedagogy with a specific focus on countering messages about distrust, disdain, and disregard. These messages are replaced with intentional sensemaking, discourse, and action that extols the brilliance, dignity, and morality of Black minds.

Personal Story – Boys Will be Boys

Our family lived in Hayward, CA, and in the late 1980s, the city was struck hard with the influx of crack cocaine. The park near our home turned from a lovely playground to a war zone for local drug dealers; soon thereafter, our neighborhood was torn apart. Our parents decided to leave. Our grandparents had spent much time in far Northern California, and our parents believed that a transition to a smaller environment would be healthier. In 1990, we moved from the Bay Area to a lumber town called McCloud. McCloud is located about an hour south of the Oregon border and nestled at the base of Mt. Shasta. McCloud was a small town with no stoplights, no movie theater, and only 1,600 people. The locals joked that this number included "cats and dogs," and I think it is safe to say the population was far smaller. The culture of the town was vastly different than the city we were from. There was a sense of trust and community. McCloud is a place where houses remain unlocked, cars are left unlocked with the keys in the ignition, and where everyone knows when something occurs. Community festivals brought families together, community theater was esteemed, and patriotism was held to be almost as sacred as God. But, among all these vestiges of culture, a pride in a long tradition of logging was central, so much so that the high school mascot was the "Logger" (and another nearby town was the "Lumberjacks"). Great grandparents, grandparents, and parents had poured their blood, sweat, and tears into the industry. The community was remnant of a lost era in history, which included both the good and the bad.

Like most towns in the Pacific Northwest, McCloud was comprised of a homogenous racial population. The vast majority of McCloudites were White, and the town had a long history of racial tension and staunch segregation endemic to the region. In fact, the town was only 30 minutes from the last reported lynching in California. Patterns of de jure housing segregation were still evident. For example, one section of town had an aging population of African Americans who had worked in the lumber mill. This part of town was known to the few remaining African Americans as "Beaumont" (I have heard this was because many of the resident's families had hailed from Beaumont, TX) and to the town Whites as "Black Town."

By the time we moved to McCloud, the lumber industry was on a downward trend, the mill was running on a skeleton crew, and increasing environmental protections threatened closure of the primary driver of the local economy. One environmental protection sought to save the spotted owl from extinction. The owl had been widespread in the region but was near extinction due to the practice of clear cutting. Clear cutting occurs when loggers cut all the trees down in a given area as opposed to cutting down selected trees in a specific area (i.e., selective cutting). This practice devastated landscapes and microenvironments and led the industry to becoming villainized. Of course, this practice was advanced by greedy owners, not by the loggers themselves, who were often very good, well-intentioned people. With impending restrictions, the move to close logging in the area sent hundreds of loggers into the woods at night to hunt and kill the owl, lest the "damn environmental tree huggers" find remaining owls in the region and restrict more areas from logging. The loggers were on the wrong end of a losing battle. Eventually, the environmentalists succeeded in forcing the closure of the mill, and this forced many families to move. While many families continued to thrive after the mill closure, some of those who remained transitioned from the working class to unemployment, and some, eventually, to welfare.

It was this background that set the context for how my experiences in school began. Like many small towns, the options for education are limited. McCloud had one K-8 school and one high school. Both resided on properties next to the other. We moved to McCloud during the summer leading up to first grade. My brother and I were the only African Americans in the school at the time. Our first-grade teacher was Mrs. D., an Italian woman who was strict and *incredibly* loving. I felt empowered to do well and developed a love for learning that was fostered under her apt tutelage. I noticed that, while children would play with me at school, we were rarely invited to their homes to play. One day, I asked my closest friend if I could come play at his house, and he said his parents would not allow "a Black" to go to his home. Similar conversations occurred with other children. I was constantly cognizant that I was different than the other children, a feeling that grew more over time.

As time passed, my love for learning deepened. I was naturally gifted at school, and I liked to learn and found it enjoyable. In contrast, social relationships with other children were often curbed by racial differences. My feeling of isolation may have been greater had I not had a twin brother. But, my focus was not on social relationships with my peers; rather, I was focused on writing. Even as a child, I wrote incessantly, particularly short stories. I excelled in English and poured my time into an area where I could be the most competitive—school. Upon entry into fourth grade, this practice seemed to be working for me. This is when things began to change with some of my male peers. Their antipathy toward my brother and me became increasingly vocalized. "Nigger," "niglet," "cottonhead," and "colored" were words that were used to refer to us on a daily basis. In fact, numerous derivations of these words were also employed, as the minds of children can be very creative.

Vocalized racism soon expanded to physical harassment, particularly after school. My brother and I would wait by the door at the end of the day to leave school as quickly as we could. When the bell would ring, we would run as fast as we could for our bikes, hop on them and pedal home with all our might. Any misstep in this process would be met with brute force, for behind us would be a group of five or six boys who would try to catch us. When they did, they would proceed to punch us, kick us, and stomp us in unison. Some have asked me why we did not fight back, but we could not—we were too busy covering our heads in our hands. Any physical counterattack on any given day was paid in even more brutal force the following day. Our parents were quite aware of the circumstance, but they simply did not know how to address what they did not want to acknowledge—the existence of virulent racism. Eventually, they had to change their position.

About halfway through the year, the group of young boys who were attacking us finally recognized that they could have greater success if they prevented us from reaching our bikes. During lunch one day, they had another child steal our bikes and ditch them off deep in the forest. Our parents saw this as an escalation and asked for a meeting with the principal. The principal met with us and our parents. They argued that this was racism and that he needed to create a safer environment for us. He noted that he could not control what takes place after school. He also stated that they were "blowing things out of proportion" and retorted that "boys will be boys." This statement, "boys will be boys," has always stuck with me. It is a saying that I detest to my core, because it represents a dismissal of injustice based upon an archaic understanding of masculinity. The next week we were informed about the location of our bikes, the only interceding he ever did. Raising the issue to the principal only served to anger the boys further. Prior to then, all altercations had occurred outside of school. From then forward, the classroom, the hallway, and the playground were no longer safe.

My self-hatred grew, even to the point that I wished I was something different, anything other than being Black. After watching the movie Queen about a mixed race slave who negotiated part of her life by appearing as White, I considered the possibility of trying to pass as White myself. I knew that my light skin was adjoined with afro-textured hair. I began to straighten my hair to erase my "cottonhead." I did this several times, sometimes completely straightened and at times loosely straightened. Ultimatley, I found that I only looked silly doing this and that my internal hurt was not similarly loosened. Once I realized that no hair product could ever change how I was received by others, I relented from my goal of being White.

I do want to acknowledge that my experiences in McCloud were not all bad. In fact, McCloud is one of the most beautiful and healthy places where a child could be raised. For every person who I met that was an outright racist, there were two others who were loving, kind, and authentic individuals. Still for me, McCloud represented a tale of two cities, one that was beautiful and healthy and the other that was marked by racism and hurt. The juxtaposition between fifth and sixth grade helps to convey the dichotomy between groups.

CHAPTER 4

BLACK MORALITY

You shouldn't have to go to prison to learn to read and to learn about yourself.
— Jawanza Kunjufu, CEO of African American Images
(Statement from Black Minds Matter)

Given the pervasive hypercriminalization of Black males discussed in the previous chapter, a key element of Black Minds Pedagogy is to extol the morality of Black minds. This suggests that educators have a responsibility to articulate that Black people, and Black learners in particular, are inherently "good," "moral," and "upstanding." This message must be believed in and communicated through both verbal and nonverbal actions. Among other actions, this entails practices that intentionally moralize Black people in the curriculum and through discussion with others. The rationale for this approach is that Black males are so ubiquitously characterized through an assumption of criminality that there is an ethical and practical need to convey the exact opposite connotation.

An assumption of criminality is a microaggression that our Black boys and men frequently experience. It involves "assuming a person of color is dangerous, criminal, or deviant based on race" (Sue et al., 2007, p. 296). While this is certainly an experience that many people of color encounter, the combination of race and gender for Black males makes them primary targets for daily experiences with this microaggression. Black males are described by educators as "menacing," "criminal," "aggressive," "troublemakers," and "nefarious." These are the words that often encapsulate the ways in which some educators' view, frame, and subsequently engage Black boys and men. As noted, this microaggression is part of the D-three effect, one of the three primary microaggressions experienced by boys and men of color. Black males are viewed through a lens of Distrust, where there is an assumption that they are inherently criminally minded.

A key element of microaggressions is that they are often rendered unconsciously from the perpetrator to the recipient. This is not necessarily an example of someone purposely trying to mar or hurt another, but a function of the more unconscious ways that people accomplish the same ends, often unknowingly (Sue et al., 2007). Microaggressions emanate from a society rooted in racism, dehumanization, and supremacy. Assumptions of criminality manifest themselves in numerous ways throughout the educational pipeline (Harper & Wood, 2015). They account for the reasons that Black boys are excluded from learning environments via suspensions and expulsions. These assumptions also explain why Black college men report being removed from classrooms, student service offices, or other locations on campus because they are perceived by others as being "aggressive" or "threatening."

In collaboration with a colleague (see Wood & Hilton, 2013), we questioned the ways Black male morality (i.e., the act of living out ethical beliefs) is framed in larger society. Specifically, we have noted that there is a continuum on how individuals can be viewed in relation to morality. This continuum ranges from moral (being viewed as good) to immoral (being viewed as bad). Fixed between these two polarized points are amoral perceptions, where individuals are viewed as having no proclivity toward one end of the continuum or the other. For Black boys and men, popular depictions of them in the media often reside somewhere between immoral perceptions to amoral perceptions at best. For example, it is not uncommon for Black males to occupy roles as gangsters, pimps, drug dealers, and brutes in film. Moreover, we argued that these stereotypes shape both societal perceptions of Black males and influence their own identity development. Possibly, this is why Ford and Harris III (1997) contend that Black male students and students who are underperforming often have less positive racial identities than their peers.

Nine Patterns of Distrust for Black Males
- Subject to continuous surveillance
- Engaged with a sense of caution
- Being singled-out for discipline
- Recipients of harsher punishments (often for minor actions)
- Mis-identified when no wrongdoing has occurred
- Recipients of quicker punishments
- Degraded and disrespected for perceived slights
- Subject to reverse causality
- Actions viewed through a disorder-based lens

Throughout the educational pipeline, the perception of criminality is evident. As such, it is not surprising that Black males are overexposed to discipline and exclusionary discipline. Here, discipline refers to punishments for wrongdoing that do not separate students from learning environments—for example, being written up or censured, put on probation, or placed in special education, school service, detention, or deferred separation (i.e., delayed suspension through a contract). In contrast, exclusionary discipline "involves the removing of students from classroom learning environments as a form of punishment" (Wood et al., 2018, p. 1). This can include, but is certainly not limited to, in-school suspensions, out-of-school suspensions, and expulsions.

Another type of exclusionary discipline less traditionally considered within this category is restriction from recess. From my perspective, recess is a critical socioemotional and physical learning environment that is central to students holistic learning and development. Given these various forms of punishment, there are numerous ways that educators can discipline Black males. In my studies with Frank Harris III and Idara Essien, we have uncovered nine primary ways in which an assumption of criminality manifests for Black boys and young men. These represent the patterns associated with the identification of disciplinary problems for Black boys and the ways educators determine which of the innumerable disciplinary tools at their disposal to apply.

In college and university settings, we often seen challenges with how Black students negotiate the campus environment (J. E. Davis, 1994). Specifically, we see criminalized perceptions of Black men manifested in how they describe their experiences with surveillance on college campuses. For instance, Black men often report to us that they are followed around campus bookstores for fear they are there to steal something. Our participants also illuminated that some Black males are asked for their IDs on campus (particularly in the evenings) to ensure that they are college students and not on the campus to vandalize property or hurt someone. This criminalized view of Black men illuminates how continuous surveillance on campus serves to paint an image of Black males as threats. The following excerpt helps to connote this experience.

> I did not have a car last semester, so I had to wait until a friend got out of class so I could get a ride home. Typically, I would get something to eat between the time that my class got out and theirs did. After that, I would go and wait in the library and spend some time studying. Frequently, the security would come to my cubicle and ask for my identification. I didn't really pay any mind to this, as I thought this was something routine. Then, one day I noticed that I was the only one being asked for their ID, so I pressed the office to see why I was being asked to show my ID but no one else was. He informed me that I fit the description of someone who they had received complaints about. That's when I stopped going to the library, it wasn't safe and I wasn't going to put myself in a position to be mistaken for someone else.† (Wood & Harris III, 2017b)

Our research has also shown that educators regularly engage Black males with a sense of caution. For instance, Black males fall victim to engagements with faculty that illustrate a greater desire to be at "safe" distances from them. For instance, Black men have remarked that faculty members will often open doors when Black male students enter into their offices or leave classroom doors open when they are with Black male students alone. As a practice, leaving a door open when alone with students is a good and professional approach in many instances. However, what Black men have reported is that the doors remain closed when other students are engaging with faculty and only left open when it is for them. Students have expressed aloud that they wonder what it is about them that reminds faculty to open doors (Wood & Harris III, 2017b). Another instance of distancing is the "step back." A step back occurs when an educator is approached by a Black male, typically after a class session has ended, and, as the student is approached, they step backwards out of socially programmed feared of that individual. This is often done unconsciously and very subtly, and the educator wonders whether the student has recognized whether the action occurred (Wood et al., 2017).

These patterns begin long before students' experiences in college, going as far back as their most formative experiences in education—beginning in preschool. Essien (2012) has examined the manifestation of microaggressions in early childhood education, with a focus on Black learners. In her work, she describes how Black males can be singled out for discipline. She presents narratives from the parents of Black children who note that their children are routinely portrayed as aggressive, disruptive, or inattentive, even in circumstances when similar behavior is manifested in other children in school settings. Other common examples of a double standard often occur on the playground where two boys who are highly active are viewed differently—one being described by educators as "energetic" while the other is portrayed as "defiant and hyperactive." As part of this study, one parent of a first-grade student shared:

> My son is the only Black child among his two close friends. When involved in an incident where the three boys were goofing off during class, my son was the only one sent to the principal's office by his teacher. (Essien, 2012, p. 8)

In addition to being singled out, research has shown that Black boys receive harsher punishments—even for minor, innocuous actions. For instance, Essien and I found that the parents of Black sons noted that this occurred regularly. For instance, the parent stated:

> My son's teacher would use severe punishments for small infractions that didn't match the crime. In fact, she would call home to report each. She called one time because he had turned around in his seat, and that resulted in him being marked the whole day as bad. But what she was doing, was she was prolonging the issue. She was punishing him and holding onto it, rather than dealing with it and moving on. I am doubtful that he got what he needed that year.† (Essien & Wood, 2018a, p. 14)

Research from Gilliam et al. (2016) helps to demonstrate that Black boys are assumed to be aberrant. Gilliam and colleagues provided teachers with video clips of White and Black children in school. In preparing the teachers for the experiment, they emphasized that a large portion of bad behavior can be identified before it occurs and gets too far out of hand. They asked teachers to watch video clips for issues that they might see unfolding. Their research found that the teachers spent more time watching Black children than White children, as they were predisposed to looking for bad behavior in this population. Interestingly, the study was a deception study, meaning that the information given to participants about the study was not fully accurate. It turns out that the clips did not depict actual issues unfolding; instead, they were simply clips of children engaged in normal behavior. It is data like these that help to demonstrate why some Black males report being (a) misidentified for discipline in circumstances where no wrong doing actually occurred; (b) subjected to quicker punishments with fewer opportunities, if any, for explanation; (c) treated with disrespect and degraded by educators when they are assumed to have done wrong; and (d) questioned and interrogated by educators after they report being mistreated because it is assumed they perpetrated some action to cause the event (e.g., reverse causality).

Beyond this, a salient pattern in the experience of Black males is being viewed through a disorder-based lens. Through this perspective, Black male actions are not simply criminalized but viewed as being a function of an erroneous psychological disorder. The disorder-based lens has its roots in the depraved, carnal, and barbarous ways that Black men have been portrayed in the popular media. As noted earlier, this depiction in film begins as early as the blockbuster movie *Birth of a Nation* that unabashedly portrayed Black males as criminal psychopaths guided by an innate malintent. In schools, this same perception can play out, with Black boys being assumed to have a similar malintent. For instance, a parent in my study with Essien stated:

> My sons' teacher yelled at him one day because he didn't put his head down. Then, she called me and told me that I should apply for funding for social security for him, and that he needs a mental evaluation because there is something not clicking in his head.† (Essien & Wood, 2018a)

The aforementioned patterns evident in the distrust of Black males requires a pedagogical practice that intentionally countermessages notions of hypercriminality. Several practices educators can employ to extol the morality of Black boys and young men include racial consciousness, moralizing, nonconfrontational tones, allowing fresh starts, and giving critique privately and praise publicly.

Racial Consciousness

Racial consciousness refers to being cognizant of race and racism at all times and how these factors influence individuals in the learning environment (Bensimon, 2007). This perspective must be situated as a lens for viewing all interactions and exchanges in educational settings. Moreover, racial consciousness is an essential framework for all discussion and actions relative to serving Black males. Being racially conscious also involves being reflective of events and actions after they have occurred, making sense of issues and patterns through this lens. Through this vigilant awareness of the deeply embedded ways Black males are hypercriminalized, educators will be more aware of how to address disproportionate discipline before it occurs.

One key strategy for being race conscious is to proactively reject deficit notions and fears of Black minds. Therefore, educators must first know how patterns of distrust manifest (e.g., being singled out, subject to reverse causality, subject to continuous surveillance). Then, this knowledge needs to be applied to individual educator's personal lens to proactively avoid repeating the same patterns. For many educators, being race conscious is a very difficult enterprise. Given that the vast majority of educators are White, these educators do not share the same racial/ethnic heritage or social experiences as Black males. Therefore, they need to be engaged in an effort to be conscious about challenges that do not affect them directly. It is certainly difficult to be aware of what you do not see or feel personally. Therefore, there may be a need for intentional strategies to ensure that being racially conscious is central in one's own mind. One strategy may be to engage in ongoing reading about the Black male experience. There has been an explosive body of research on Black males in education since the 1990s (e.g., Bonner, Jennings, Marbley, & Brown, 2008; Dancy, 2014; Ford & Moore, 2013; Harper, 2014; Strayhorn & Tillman-Kelly, 2013); this research can be used as a guide for a deeper and continued understanding of the Black male experience. Participation in professional learning communities focused or organized around Black males can also support vigilance around issues of hypercriminality.

Rejecting deficit notions requires and advanced understanding of the challenges facing Black males. One key strategy for creating awareness is to participate in trainings on unconscious bias, racial microaggressions, and teaching practices for boys and men of color. One key resource is the Center for Organizational Responsibility and Advancement (CORA) that specializes in in-person and online training for educators on these topics. The organization, of which I am a co-director, provides these topical trainings with a specific focus on Black boys and men throughout the educational pipeline. While CORA is a leading resource, there are other training and development organizations, conferences, and symposia designed to better prepare educators for these issues.

In addition to training, being race conscious also requires being hands-on in gaining a greater feel for the issues facing Black boys and men in educators' own settings. Every institution of learning—from preschool to doctoral education—has some type of data collection on discipline. This could include data from school and college districts, state boards, governing bodies, and government agencies. Educators must become familiar with data on students in their schools and take personal responsibility for these outcomes, regardless of whether they have personally contributed to the disproportionality that will almost certainly be readily identifiable. Armed with this data, educators can hold themselves and their colleagues accountable for employing fair and consistent practices that do not "target" Black males and, instead, communicate their morality.

Moralizing

While vigilance is essential in and of itself, vigilance is not effective enough for countering the pervasive and deeply seeded ways that Black males are hypercriminalized. Therefore, educators must engage in moralizing practices. Moralizing practices refer to efforts that ensure that the curriculum, examples provided in the classroom, and discussion are culturally relevant, while also proactively affirming the morality and inherent dignity of Black minds. One moralizing strategy can include presenting Black boys and men in moralized ways in the curriculum. The curriculum in many schools, colleges, and universities either ignores Black males or presents them in stereotypical ways (e.g., as athletes, entertainers, criminals). Outside of passing references (during Black History Month) to Martin Luther King Jr., Rosa Parks, and Frederick Douglas, there are few examples where the curriculum does not ignore Black people. Even when educators attempt to be culturally relevant, they often select books that portray Black males as individuals who are nefarious, overcoming past criminal history, or coming from gang-riddled neighborhoods. Therefore, it is not enough to be culturally relevant—an added focus must be on emphasizing Black morality.

As such, identifying books, readings, and lecture materials that depict Black people, history, and culture in moral ways is essential. This can include fiction and nonfiction readings where Black males are advocates for a more just society, demonstrate acts of selflessness, dedicate their lives to service, and exemplify qualities of moral leaders.

Further, when classroom discussions occur, educators must also reject deficit notions and fears of Black males. It is not uncommon for students at all ages to tacitly accept the ubiquitous societal stereotypes of Black males as criminals. This tacit acceptance can emerge from the subtle ways that Black males are framed in discourse in the classroom. This can include statements such as, "Many of them come from bad communities," "Black people are more likely to be criminals," references to Black men as dangerous, and more vicious responses to Black men who have committed criminal acts than are given in response to other groups. As part of being racially conscious, educators should identify these references when they occur. When doing so, educators must respond by countering these notions, offering different perspectives and challenging students to see the world in the different way.

It should be noted that rejecting deficit notions and fears is not limited to educators' interactions with students. Rather, these same notions are also extended by parent volunteers, classroom aids, and peer teachers. Informed by Bensimon's (2007) work on equity-mindedness, I believe that educators have a responsibility to hold their colleagues accountable for the ways they talk about and engage Black males. This is a difficult enterprise for many educators, because there is often a desire to avoid being confrontational or to display dissension. Even when this occurs in polite ways that are designed to support others' learning and development, there may be a sense of awkwardness associated with holding colleagues accountable. Moreover, there are certainly some colleagues who are not open to hearing how their words and actions are harmful to Black males. That being said, the responsibility remains. As such, educators must find ways to extend these messages, especially when it is uncomfortable to do so.

As part of holding colleagues accountable, educators can also signal different ways of thinking about Black males by fostering counternarratives that moralize them. Specifically, this involves discussing Black male learners in ways that intentionally highlight that they are "good," "moral," and "upstanding." This can serve to frame Black males differently in the minds of those who may tacitly ascribe to societal stereotypes about them. For example, let's say that two educators are engaged in a conversation about a Black male. One who embraces Black Minds Pedagogy can offer very specific insights and examples on the myriad ways the student is moral. This could include statements such as, "He is a really nice young man," "I'm so proud of him—he is such a caring person," "He is a leader with immense integrity," or "Our society is in good hands with upstanding young men like him."

Offering such counternarratives can increase the likelihood that other educators will see the student differently—to see them as human. As part of emphasizing language that moralizes Black males, educators must also be careful not to label Black males who (like all other students) may commit acts that transgress expected rules and policies. In such cases, there should be a focus on the action and an avoidance of labeling behavior. The nuance here may sound somewhat trite; however, actions speak more clearly to what one has done. In contrast, behavior can insinuate a deeper disposition toward certain actions. Therefore, there is a need to relanguage even the subtle ways that educators talk about Black boys and young men.

Nonconfrontational Tones

To teach Black males differently, educators must think about them differently (rejecting deficit notions) and talk about them differently (moralizing practices); they must also engage them differently. The next three recommended practices are emblematic of this important influence on the translation between thoughts and actions. First, let us examine the use of nonconfrontational tones.

Nonconfrontational tones refers to using language that is "calm, non-hostile, and respectful" (Wood & Harris III, 2017a, p. 75) when engaging Black boys and young men. Nonconfrontational tones are inclusive of both verbal and nonverbal communication that demonstrates a welcoming and friendly demeanor. While this practice is necessary for all aspects of the educational experience, there is a need to engage this practice when some form of corrective intervention is occurring. Corrective action is essential in any educational setting, serving as a mechanism for communicating normative expectations around relationships, academic engagement, classroom behavior, and more. The rationale for this approach is that educators often speak to and engage with Black boys in an overly aggressive and defensive posture. This is particularly true when educators perceive that some wrongdoing has occurred (e.g., being disruptive, arguing, inattentiveness). This is due to the embedded fears of Black males, the pervasive dehumanization, and the hypercriminalized ways that Black males are viewed. For Black males, each subsequent experience is filtered through the lens of similarly negative experiences.

These perspectives have contributed to the reasons Black boys and young men often feel minoritized, alienated, and uncared for in educational settings. At a minimum, this should include speaking in a caring voice and maintaining a peaceful disposition. Engaging Black males in this way, particularly during corrective action, is essential because this practice demonstrates respect in a manner that disrupts dismissive narratives about Black males. This is important for Black males to experience and for their peers to see. Moreover, when not engaged in this manner, some Black males will reciprocate the negative ethos they have encountered. I believe this may be a necessary defense mechanism to guard against further racial harm. Unfortunately, in some circumstances, the accumulation of these responses between educators and students can only serve to escalate an experience.

Allowing Fresh Starts

It is critical that educators allow for a fresh start—"treating each day as a new day" (Wood & Harris III, 2017a, p. 77). This suggests that educators engage Black males each day without harboring ongoing resentment against them for previous actions. The privilege of a fresh start is necessary for providing a healthy learning environment where children can thrive intellectually, socially, and emotionally. Moreover, this privilege is readily extended to other children, but often withheld from Black boys. Thus, educators must simply be willing to provide Black boys with a fresh start, as they would with any other child. But, unlike other children, educators need to be proactive in recognizing the need to do so and executing actions that are associated with this perspective.

In Wood and Harris III (2017b), we identified K-12 educators with a proven record of success in teaching boys and young men of color, particularly Black and Latino males. A clear theme from that project was that exemplar teachers approached classroom management by treating each day as a fresh start. In the study, one teacher remarked that other educators must recognize this:

> Each day is a new day. Unfortunately, there is a stigma that follows boys of color throughout their school careers, especially if they have had discipline issues in the past. Some students will have reputations that precede them. I tell my students that each day is a new day. What you may have done yesterday has nothing to do with how you will be treated by me today. Each day is a new opportunity to do better. (Wood & Harris, 2017b, p. 77)

In Chapter 2, we discussed the adultification of Black boys, noting how they often experience a denial of youthfulness. One aspect of this pattern is that Black boys are often not given the benefit of the doubt, or seen as innocent, in need of nurturance, or in need of protection. They are not perceived as a child making a mistake, but as an adult with nefarious intentions. Goff et al. (2014) provided this example:

> A man who makes a mistake is perceived as knowing better and thus deserves a more rigorous punishment and is not immediately deserving of forgiveness [while] a child who makes a mistake is merely seen as a kid who is learning. (p. 77)

As such, if an actual or perceived wrongdoing has occurred, Black boys are assumed to have malintent. This results in the actions being viewed differently and as deserving of punishment, rather than a learning moment. Given this, it is not uncommon for Black boys to be restricted from having a fresh start the following day. This pattern, while evident in early childhood, can continue with Black boys throughout their educational careers. This also connects to the nine patterns of Black male criminalization (e.g., subject to continuous surveillance, engaged with a sense of caution, recipients of harsher punishments) discussed in Chapter 4. While this experience certainly begins in early childhood education, even doctoral students can experience "predisposed grudge-holding" from faculty. For example, I have witnessed Black male graduate students miss a class and a faculty member making the assumption that they are trying to "get by," "break the rules," or somehow "cheat the system."

Critique Privately, Praise Publicly

One principle of practice that can serve to extol the morality of Black males is to critique privately and praise publicly. The concept emanates from two separate studies on exemplar educators for males of color, one focused on community college instructors (see Wood et al., 2015) and the other on preK-12 education (Wood & Harris III, 2017a). In these studies, we learned lessons from teaching males of color from those who had a documented record of success in doing so. In both studies, educators noted the criticality of critiquing privately and praising publicly. This involves providing "critiques of their performance and actions in private sessions" (Wood & Harris III, 2017a, p. 78), while acknowledging positive actions and performance publicly. This practice is relevant to both teaching practices that extol the brilliance of Black males and to classroom management practices that extol their morality.

When Black males do not meet expectations (e.g., academic, conduct), they are often subject to actions that degrade or dismiss them. These actions only serve to actualize fears that many Black males harbor about their aptitude and belonging in school or college (Wood, 2014). For example, Black males are often apprehensive about asking or responding to questions in class for fear of being perceived as academically inferior. They are also hyperaware of the pervasive ways they are criminalized. Thus, lauding their positive performance or inherent upstanding character in public is essential for crafting a different narrative about them. As noted previously, this is essential for Black males in terms of how they perceive themselves. In fact, our research has indicated that public praise can serve to promote students' confidence in their academic abilities (Wood & Harris III, 2017a). However, I would argue that this is also important for how they view themselves of moral beings. Beyond this, public praise can also serve to disrupt D-three narratives that students and other educators may harbor about Black males. However, the ability of these messages to connote powerful counternarratives is dependent upon the degree to which public praise is received as authentic by Black males and their peers.

In addition to public praise, critiques about academic performance or conduct should not occur in a manner that is visible to others, when possible. Like other males, Black males desire to maintain a sense of pride and control. Their desire to do so may be particularly heightened in environments, like school, where their pride and control are often negated and regulated. For instance, one educator in a previous study noted, "Public reprimand generally results in shut down, disengagement, or disrespect. Quiet reprimand and public praise work consistently" (Wood & Harris III, 2017a, p. 83). Thus, when corrective actions are necessary, educators should do so privately. This can occur by pulling students aside, speaking with them after class, or speaking with them quietly during class. The use of nonconfrontational tones that convey respect is essential. As noted, our previous studies have demonstrated the efficacy of this approach. For example, one educator stated:

> I try to speak with individuals one on one, away from other students. This helps them to "save face" and lowers the risk that the issue will spread to the whole group. Given this, critiquing privately while also praising publicly is a practice that is good for Black males that is also beneficial for overall classroom management.† (Wood & Harris III, 2017a, p. 83).

While there are five primary strategies offered in this chapter (e.g., racial consciousness, moralizing practices, nonconfrontational tones, allowing for a fresh start, critiquing privately and praising publicly), there are many other ways educators can extol the morality of Black males. As emphasized throughout this volume, it is not enough for educators to avoid communicating distrust to Black males; there is a need to proactively foster different viewpoints, narratives, and actions that communicate the exact opposite message. This is necessary for disrupting the pervasive societal viewpoints of Black males as hypercriminalized. In the next chapter, I examine similar strategies that can counteract pervasive perceptions of Black academic inferiority.

Personal Story – Get Out!

In fifth grade, I entered the classroom with a sense of exuberance. The prior year of school had exposed me to a caring teacher, Mary Sideman, who embraced all of her students. Though I did not get to finish the year with Ms. Sideman, as she left the year early due to the birth of her child, I was flying high from my experience with her. Fifth grade was entirely another matter. My teacher that year was Ms. Harrington, a long-time teacher with a penchant for maintaining power through oppression. Simply put, she was racist. I do not describe her using these terms lightly; as an educator, I have worked arduously to elevate the ways society talks about children and their teachers. However, I would be disingenuous if I described Ms. Harrington otherwise. By the time most Black males enter this grade level, the perception of them in the minds of others has already changed. They are no longer viewed as innocent "kids" but culpable "men." Upon entry into her classroom, I became an immediate target. The children who bullied my brother and I were lauded for their efforts, and any response to their increasing audacious behavior resulted in us being singled out for discipline. We were the subject of reverse causality by being punished for speaking up, defending ourselves, or asking for help.

That year, I became part of a national pattern that affects many young boys of color: exclusionary discipline. Exclusionary discipline refers to "disciplinary practices that remove [students] from learning environments, thereby, restricting them from learning opportunities necessary for their success" (Wood & Harris III,

2017b, pp. 2-3). Examples of exclusionary discipline include the practices of suspension and expulsion. There are various forms of these practices in place in our schools today, such as in-school (or in-house) suspension where the child is relocated out of the classroom for a period of time, typically no more than a few days. Suspensions can also prevent students from attending school, ranging in time from short-term suspensions to extended or long-term suspensions. In addition, a student can be expelled from school, where they are prevented from returning to the same school or to schools within the same district (depending on the nature of the perceived behavior). One common approach used in many schools is to remove a student from their school and send them to a specialized school (such as a continuation school).

Ms. Harrington regularly suspended me from class. This included a few out-of-school suspensions, but mostly in-school suspensions. In all, I was suspended 42 times. When I speak with audiences about discipline, most people are in disbelief about this. But this was my experience—a very difficult, hurtful experience. Any perceived slight on my part would be responded to with a sense of anger, with Ms. Harrington yelling "get out" and directing me to the principal's office. They would then place me in a desk near the library where sometimes I would receive schoolwork, and other times, I would not. I sat at this desk so regularly that, at some point, I started to consider it "my desk." My twin brother was subject to the same pattern, though to a somewhat lesser degree; he was suspended only 24 times in that same year. I grew to hate school that year. I hated the students, I hated the teachers, I hated every aspect of schooling. I began to withdraw from school, crafting an identity that disassociated from learning and achievement. In one year, Ms. Harrington had stolen a fire for learning that had been present throughout my life. The fire was extinguished. I remember telling my parents how much I disliked her, how I felt targeted, and how what she was doing was wrong. They knew I was right but did not possess the tools, beyond words of support, to change what had occurred.

Around that same time, another event occurred that also affected my experience in school—the O.J. Simpson trial. In this trial, the beloved athlete turned media superstar was accused of murdering his wife and her friend. The national spotlight was on this event. The media could not resist the ratings power of a large, "trusted" Black male viciously murdering his White wife. The case was not simply a "case," rather, it was courtroom theater. When the verdict was going to be read, the teachers in our school decided that the students could not miss out on this important moment in history. They thought it would be more "educational" for us to watch the verdict being read in real-time, so they brought many of the students to the school library to watch and hear the verdict being read on the television. I remember sitting in the room when this occurred, listening intently, watching the body language of people in the courtroom, and also being attentive to the dynamics of my peers and teachers in the library. People talked openly about their perceptions of his guilt; it was generally assumed that we were there to watch his conviction. However, what was supposed to be a public lynching did not occur. Due to the incredible judicial wizardry of Johnny Cochrane, O.J. was acquitted. I remember, as the verdict was being read, the gasps in the room, the immediate turn to palpable anger, and the pursuant racialized and animalistic references to O.J. Simpson, Black males, and the Black community in general. This was an incredibly isolating incident, as their expression of frustration only served to illuminate the racial divide between myself, my teachers, and my peers. For me, it was certainly an educational moment, just not the one the teachers intended.

Some names have been changed.

CHAPTER 5

BLACK BRILLIANCE

If you don't believe in them, how do you expect them to see themselves as gifted?
— Fred Bonner II, Endowed Professor,
Prairie View A & M University

Special education is not that special, or you'd see more Whites in it.
— Donna Ford, Endowed Professor,
Vanderbilt University

Black males are forced to prove where others' abilities and capacities are assumed.
— Kimberly A. Griffin, Associate Professor,
University of Maryland
(Statements from Black Minds Matter)

A key component of Black Minds Pedagogy is to extol the brilliance of Black minds. This is meant to counter pervasive messages that Black learners receive from educators, peers, family, and society at large that communicate their inability to succeed academically. With respect to the D-three effect, extolling brilliance is a direct response to the disregard often communicated to Black boys and men. This aligns with a concept called *ascription of intelligence* that Sue et al. (2007) proffered. Sue, one of the most prominent psychologists in the nation, extended previous work on microaggressions to offer a taxonomy of the primary ways that people of color are slighted in society. His work centers on the very subtle ways that people of color are demeaned, degraded, and insulted by Whites. Within Sue's taxonomy, ascription of intelligence refers to the act of "assigning intelligence to a person of color on the basis of their race" (Sue et al., 2007, p. 296). This entails making assumptions about a person's ability, or lack thereof, solely upon their racial identity. For some individuals, these assumptions may infer that they are of high academic ability. However, for Black boys and men, the assumption is that they are inherently incapable of success. These perceptions are held by educators, peers, and sometimes by Black students themselves.

One of the most common examples given of this type of microaggression is a person of color being told with a sense of surprise that they are well spoken, intelligent, or capable. When combined with a sense of surprise, a comment that is intended to be a compliment becomes an insult. Research has repeatedly shown that Black learners are subject to these well-intended but harmful compliments (e.g., "Wow, you are very well spoken!," "You are really smart!," "How did you know that?!"). Another example of this type of microaggression can occur on the first day of class at a college or university. A student may walk into a classroom for the first time and be greeted by a kind-hearted faculty member who assumes that, because of the color of their skin, they may be in the wrong classroom. The faculty member may respond, "What room are you looking for? This is organic chemistry." Their intention may be to be assistive and help the student find their classroom. However, for a student who is actually enrolled in the class, the faculty has communicated that they do not belong because they made an assumption that they were in the wrong room. Again, like other microaggressions, these messages are often rendered unintentionally, but they are still harmful.

While students can be microaggressed from their faculty, they can also be microaggressed by their peers. In Wood et al. (2015), we discussed the fact that collaborative learning can often serve as an instance where microaggressions are manifested. Faculty may encourage students to work in groups of their own design; however, we showed that Black men are often the last to be picked or, in many cases, not picked at all for small groups. If they are picked, it can occur with a sense of reluctance or body language that communicates a sense of disappointment with the pairing.

Five Patterns of Disregard for Black Males
- A sense of surprise when Black boys and men are intelligent
- Avoidance of collaborative group-work by peers
- Educators viewing breakdowns in performance from a disorder-based lens
- Second-guessing excellence when it occurs
- Slower to acknowledge and praise

A disregard for Black minds begins early. For example, Essien (2012) documented microaggressions occurring in early childhood education. She cited instances where preschool teachers communicated a sense of surprise to parents about their children's articulation and cognitive assets. These messages only serve to reinforce ascriptions of intelligence and can influence the ways Black learners engage in the classroom.

One of the studies I conducted helped to examine the ways that widely held perceptions of Black academic inferiority affect learners. The article, "Apprehension to Engage in the Community College Classroom," was based on my dissertation research where I conducted interviews with 28 African American men attending a community college located in the Southwestern United States (Wood, 2014). In the study, I asked the interviewees to tell me about their experiences in school and the factors that served to influence their success. As part of the interviews, a consistent response from many of the men was that their success was influenced by their engagement. Specifically, students noted that they were cautious about engaging in and out of the classroom.

It was disheartening to hear from so many students that they restricted their involvement in the classroom. Students noted that faculty members would pose questions to the class to see if students had correct responses; however, the men stated that they would oftentimes know the answer but would not say anything. Students also noted that, after covering new material during a lecture, faculty would ask whether students had any questions. They commented that they would have questions to which they really needed answer, but they withheld from asking them. Beyond this, students stated that faculty members would remind students of their office hours and invite students to come and get additional support if they needed. Students remarked that they knew they needed to attend but refrained from doing so. These men were not disengaged, or uncaring, or unmotivated—rather, they were apprehensive to engage (Wood, 2014).

As a follow-up to their comments, I often asked the students why they chose not to engage. Each time, the response was very clear. They were worried the faculty members and their peers would perceive them as being "dumb," "unintelligent," "ignorant," and "stupid." These learners were terrified of communicating anything that might serve to reinforce the widely held perception that they were academically inferior, and thus, did not belong in the classroom. This apprehension to engage aligns with research from Claude Steele (1997) on stereotype threat. Stereotype threat occurs when learners become concerned about reaffirming negative stereotypes about themselves. Much of the early work on stereotype threat focused on how Black and Latinx learners were concerned that they would affirm stereotypes about their inferiority.

As with any student group, there are some Black boys and men who may struggle in the classroom. This can be due to a litany of factors, such as prior preparation, the disposition of the teacher, external pressures, or a culturally isolating curriculum. Regardless of why this can occur, it is clear that the ways academic breakdowns are rationalized differ across racial/ethnic groups. Specifically, when breakdowns in performance occur among Black learners, many educators view the challenge through a disorder-based lens. They seek to understand the type of mental impairment that may be inhibiting the student from being successful. In contrast, other students experiencing the same concerns are examined more holistically, without an immediate assumption that something is wrong with their mental capacity. An unfortunate outgrowth of these differential perspectives is that Black boys and men are too often referred to special education to receive services they do not need.

While special education is a critical service for those who are in need of specialized support, special education is a "dumping ground" for far too many Black boys and men. It represents a place where they can be sent that absolves their teachers of any responsibility for their learning, development, and success.

Another key way that an ascription of intelligence can manifest is by second-guessing excellence when it occurs. In 2016, I co-authored an article in the *Huffington Post* with Frank Harris III titled, "Too Smart to Succeed, Too Good to Win." The article was based on our research and observations on Black learners and professionals. Essentially, the article highlighted what occurs when students outperform low expectations. In our research, we found that when Black males performed well on tests, assignments, and papers in classrooms where teachers assumed they were incapable of doing so, the immediate response was to assume they had somehow cheated or cut corners. As such, when Black males outperform low expectations, the response by some educators is not to raise expectations, but instead, to elevate their scrutiny.

An ascription of intelligence can also occur when educators are slower to acknowledge and praise Black boys and men. Being slower to acknowledge them can be a function of overlooking them because of unconscious assumptions about their intelligence, more carefully vetting their academic assets, or simply not placing high regard on their abilities. Essien and I examined microaggressions experienced by Black boys in early childhood education (Essien & Wood, 2018b). In this study, we asked parents to describe the racialized experiences they and their children had with educators while their children were progressing through early learning. A quote from the study helps to demonstrate the salience of this issue of being slower to acknowledge and praise. One parent stated the following:

> In second grade, my son's teacher refused to acknowledge that my son was intelligent, despite the fact that he was one of the smartest kids in her class. Throughout the year, students received awards that recognized their achievements based on the grades they had earned. During the ceremony, the teacher made sure to give awards out to all of the White children with pride and smiles on her face. In fact, she even gave a little speech about each child, talking about how great they were. Then, when my Black son's name was called, it was totally different. There was no excitement, no speech, and no words. He was just handed his award and that was it. (Essien & Wood, 2018b, slide 15)

Consider how detrimental these interactions could be. Black Minds Pedagogy intentionally counters these pervasive messages of academic inferiority in several critical ways, including culturally affirming practices, validating messages, mirror artifacts, leadership opportunities, and conveying high expectations.

Culturally Affirming Practices

Culturally affirming practices ensure that the curriculum is relevant to the lived sociocultural experiences of students, while proactively affirming the brilliance of Black minds. Therefore, being culturally responsive is not enough, as the goal is to advance a counternarrative that centers Blacks as purveyors of knowledge and sources of intelligence. Thus, culturally affirming practices are relevant with the intended purpose of advancing this atypical narrative about Black minds.

Culturally affirming practices should honor both the historical and contemporary contributions of Black people. There are numerous historical figures from the Black community who have contributed to knowledge in every discipline. Their contributions are often unheralded or altogether ignored. Students should be equally exposed to influences of Black inventors, academicians, technologists, and theoreticians as they are to those who are non-Black. There are numerous examples of key figures who should be recognized in the curriculum, such as Charles Drew, Elijah McCoy, Granville Woods, Frederick Douglas, W.E.B. Dubois, Garrett Morgan, Alexander Miles, and Benjamin Montgomery. Likely, those reading this have only heard of a few of these names, which is a testament to the inadequacy of our current educational system.

As such, Black students leave most classrooms being able to offer concrete examples of how non-Black leaders have contributed to knowledge, but are unable to recall even a few who are Black. This is egregious and an example of the pervasive symbolic violence that tacitly advances scripts that subjugate Black learners in the classroom. Even in classrooms where Black individuals are accounted for in the curriculum, the manner in which this is done often misses the mark. Specifically, Wood et al. (2015) argued that educators should avoid positioning Black history as solely limited to slavery, emancipation, and the Civil Rights Movement. This is due to the fact that this approach relegates Black contributions to finite points in history, washing away the collective advances of the community that fall outside these two points in time.

While concepts, ideas, and innovations should be presented in a historical perspective that centers Black people in the classroom, there is also a need to use contemporary examples to accomplish the same end. This is an essential practice for ensuring that students feel that issues relevant to their lives, interests, and culture are honored in the classroom. When presenting information on any topic, educators can provide current examples on how Black people have: (a) contributed to contemporary advancements, and/or (b) used the concepts that are being discussed in class in their work. This should go beyond using illustrations to discuss course topics to being deeply reflective in course readings, assignments, lectures, and all other materials. For example, educators can identify current leaders across disciplines who have advanced previous concepts or who are using these concepts in their current practice. The power of this approach is even more evident when educators facilitate students' understanding of how course concepts relate to their personal lives.

Validating Messages

Validation is another strategy for affirming Black minds. This concept first emerged from the research of Laura Rendón (1994) when she identified the need for students of color (particularly Latinx students) to be educated in environments that validated their presence, contributions, and abilities. While Rendón's work has focused more holistically on validation as an environmental and instructional strategy, my work on validation has more closely centered on validating messages. From this perspective, validating refers to "communicating high expectations about students' abilities and aptitudes" (Wood & Harris III, 2017a, p. 46). Educators can communicate these messages by telling their students messages that motivate them to succeed (e.g., "Keep working hard, I can see the improvement," "You have the ability to do this," "Keep going strong") and that affirm their abilities (e.g., "Excellent work, "I'm proud of what you've done").

These messages, when conveyed with a deep sense of sincerity, have manifold benefits for Black males. For example, Wood and Harris III (2017a) found that Black men who were validated by educators demonstrated increased noncognitive outcomes, such as confidence in their academic abilities, perceptions of the usefulness of school, enhanced interest in academic learning, greater focus in school, and a greater sense of control over their academic futures. While these messages are simple to convey, they are too often withheld from our Black boys and men. I have often found that educators believe in students' abilities to succeed. However, I have also found that, more often than not, their belief is not readily communicated to students. Instead, it is assumed and taken for granted that students know that educators believe in them. It is imperative that educators convey these messages to students.

Interestingly, Black males who do receive messages of validation in school and college settings often do not report receiving these messages from classroom teachers and faculty. In fact, outside of the classroom, males of color, in general, report that they have few interactions, if any, with their instructors. They note that, when they see their faculty members, the faculty members walk the other direction, put their heads down, and pretend to be on the phone to avoid interacting with Black males. Instead, research from Wood et al. (2015) found that Black men reported having stronger relationships with noninstructional educators. In particular, they found that janitors, custodians, food service workers, and groundskeepers were the individuals from whom Black males reported hearing messages of validation. These individuals told students they were proud of them, encouraged them to keep pushing forward, extolled the importance of school, and validated their presence in school settings. This is a critical point to consider for several reasons. First, this notion should serve as motivation for all instructional faculty to be more intentional in engaging Black males and conveying messages of validation to them. Second, this point helps to demonstrate that there is a need to rid our educational institutions of hierarchies that denote certain employees as educators while assuming others are not. In reality, all individuals within an educational institution have the responsibility to affirm Black minds.

One key point to consider when engaging in validation is that there is a need to validate both effort and ability. This is a key departure from the original perspective on growth mindset proffered by Carol Dweck. Initially, Dweck (2014) argued the following:

> [We] can praise wisely, not praising intelligence or talent. That has failed. Don't do that anymore. But praising the process that kids engage in: their effort, their strategies, their focus, their perseverance, their improvement. This process praise creates kids who are hardy and resilient.

I have argued that this perspective is harmful because it assumes learners have a baseline experience with being praised for their abilities. In contrast, many Black boys and men have not experienced validation of their abilities; therefore, praising their effort only without ever conveying to them that there is an inherent belief in their capacity to perform is not fruitful. It only serves to perpetuate a myth of meritocracy. Fortunately, Dweck responded to my critique, acknowledging that there are some populations for which validation of ability and effort are necessary. For Black males, the balance of the two messages is central to their success.

Validation is most impactful when it is task-specific and tangible (Wood et al., 2015). As such, identifying specific tasks (e.g., assignments, exams, quizzes, essays) on which the student has performed well and conveying validation of their performance on these tasks is most beneficial. Even more beneficial, educators will find that validating Black males publicly in front of their peers serves a two-fold purpose. First, it elevates the contributions of Black males in the classroom, and, second, it serves to counter popular conceptions that other students may hold about their abilities that assume their inferiority. Of course, the validation must be rooted in actual performance, as false or trite validation can produce the opposite of the intended effect and lead the student to be weary of the educator.

Lastly, it is critical that educators who validate Black boys and men expect to receive "pushback." Given that many Black males have not received validation of their abilities throughout their educational experiences, it is common for an educator to validate their contributions and for that validation to be rejected or viewed cautiously. The student may ask himself, "What is their angle?," "Why are they saying this to me?," "Are they trying to get over on me?," "What do they really want?" This occurs because of the infrequency with which Black males receive these messages. Thus, it is essential that, when educators validate students, they recognize that single messages may not be received as truly validating. As such, validation should be intensive, pervasive, and ongoing to break through the emotional barriers of protection that many Black males hold.

Mirror Artifacts

Affirming Black minds requires educators to recognize the environmental factors that often ignore the value of Black males. One can walk down the hallways of any educational institution or visit the cafeteria, classrooms, and offices and find few—if any—images of Black males as learners. While schools and colleges often employ marketing materials that highlight stock images of Black males or regularly depict *the one* Black male from the campus who is literally on *all* the campus photos—this external face is not reflective of the internal walls. Images of Black males in the physical spaces, online platforms, and course materials are absent. As a result, the pervasive images of non-Black students serve to center them as learners and valued contributors.

More often than not, if a Black male is depicted, the contribution is usually limited to their athletic prowess—as members of the football team, basketball team, or track and field team. I have attended several lunches at the faculty and staff club at a university in my local area. The club is a central space on campus where professors and administrators come together over food and drinks. The walls of the club have 12 images, each in Black and White, to emphasize the history of the campus. Ten of these pictures depict the founding of the institution, campus leaders, students studying, and engagement in other academic pursuits. However, Black students (of any gender) are noticeably absent from these images. However, the remaining two images, not featured in a main room, depict two Black students, both who are student-athletes. The images show them engaged in competition, advancing the legacy of the college with contributions tied to their dominance in sports.

As I viewed these images, I have often thought to myself how these images—both what is absent and what is present—have served to shape the hearts and minds of the educators who have engaged thousands of Black students over the years. These images have reinforced popular stereotypes of Black people as having little to contribute to the educational mission beyond athletics. These images remind me of a foundational article written on students of color titled, "Guests in Someone Else's House," by Caroline Turner (1994). In her article, she noted that many students of color do not feel at home in institutions of education, but rather, they feel like guests. Turner (1994) stated:

> Like students of color in the university climate, guests have no history in the house they occupy. There are no photographs on the wall that reflect their image. Their paraphernalia, paintings, scents, and sounds do not appear in the house. There are many barriers for students who constantly occupy a guest status. (p. 356)

A couple years ago, I gave a speech about men of color at a community college located in Southern California, and, something happened that has resonated with me ever since. It was the first time I can remember feeling an overwhelming sense that I was at home and *not a guest*. As I walked into the room, I noticed that the walls were covered with images of Black leaders, both past and present. The images left little space on the walls, demarcating the room as Black centric. The conversation among all the individuals in the room centered around how empowered we felt. Our spirits were lifted, we felt valued, powerful, enlivened, and excited for our discussion. I soon learned that the room was often used by the campus' Black studies program. I felt a deep sense of contentment that the Black students who entered this classroom had at least one space where they were no longer guests, but were at home. I wondered to myself how different schools and colleges would feel if the walls and halls were more reflective of the diversity of students, rather than presenting a myopic depiction of Whiteness. Would students perform better? Would they feel a greater sense of connection to the campus? Would they be more confident?

Along with my colleague Dr. Wendy Bracken, I set out to test the effect these images would have on students. Informed by the research on reading education, we became exposed to the concept of what are referred to as window books and mirror books. For children of color, window books are books that serve as a window into someone else's world. They represent books that have key characters, themes, and storylines that are White. These books do not reflect the realities of Black students. Instead, Black students peer through the window of their own realities into these texts. Unfortunately, and as noted earlier, the window experience is the predominant experience to which Black children are exposed. The halls they walk through, the images they see, the curriculum and the teachers, and every aspect of their schooling experience is stationed before the window. The life of peering through a window is unbearable to our Black minds. In contrast, there is another concept called mirror books. Mirror books are books that allow Black students to see reflections of themselves. These books allow Black learners to see stories, characters, and content that reflects their lived experiences and realities. What a great sense of empowerment to stand in front of the mirror and see oneself. At least, that is what we sought to uncover.

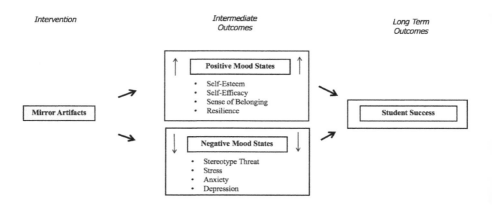

Informed by these perspectives, we offered two concepts: mirror artifacts and the mirror effect. *Mirror artifacts* refer to exposing [Black] students to racially salient images that highlight their contributions to society. Our view was that being exposed to mirror artifacts (i.e., racially salient image in the curriculum, course materials, classroom pictures) would lead to positive mood states, such as confidence in students' academic abilities, greater self-esteem, a sense of belonging, and resilience. We also supposed that mirror artifacts could lessen the harm of negative factors, such as stereotype threat, stress, and anxiety. *The mirror effect* is the term we used for this hypothesized result of mirror artifacts fostering positive mood states and limiting negative moods states.

To test this hypothesis, we sought to create a static environment where the influence of external factors could be limited. We began with online testing. A number of examinations have been conducted using this process, and I will describe two here. In the first study, we exposed Black graduate students to an online test. In the online test, students were randomly assigned to two groups—one that had embedded images of Black icons (e.g., Martin Luther King, Jr., Malcolm X, Michelle Obama, and Serena Williams). The second condition (the control group) received no images at all. Individuals were provided with SAT questions that had questions embedded within them that had no correct answer. The goal was to elevate students' concerns about their abilities, being graduate students who knew they were taking the SAT, and having questions with which they struggled mightily. At the end of these questions were different assessments of their noncognitive outcomes. The first study included measures for students' state anxiety and for stereotype threat (i.e., their concerns about reifying negative stereotypes about people of color). In line with our hypothesis, we found that those who received the mirror artifacts had significantly reduced scores for anxiety. They also had a significant reduction in their stereotype threat. Why does this matter? Because it signals that the mere presence of images can create a better environment for students. Our Black males need more mirrors and less windows.

Excited about the potential of these findings, we sought to determine whether this intervention would be beneficial for other students. Our hypothesis was that White students would also benefit from an enhanced diversification of images. We expanded our pool and set our sights on a different outcome: self-efficacy. *Self-efficacy* refers to students' confidence in their ability to perform and execute academic tasks and functions. An imperfect translation is that self-efficacy encompasses students' confidence in their academic abilities. We assumed that greater confidence would be seen for both groups that were exposed to these diverse images. However, we were wrong. What we found instead is that Black students benefitted immensely from these images. When exposed to mirror artifacts, Black students became more confident in their abilities. In contrast, White students did not benefit. In fact, their confidence in their academic abilities declined, almost to the point of significance. These findings made us wonder, if this is how White students responded to diverse images, what are the long-term effects for Black students who are perpetually situated before windows throughout their educational experiences? My personal perspective is that being a guest in someone else's house is a form of symbolic violence against our Black learners.

Bearing this in mind, it is essential that educators be unapologetically intentional about extolling Black minds through mirror artifacts. These artifacts should include images in and on all the artifacts in the learning environment. These images should expose Black learners to racially salient images, particularly images of Black leadership and knowledge production that serves to affirm Black minds by centering them as key purveyors of knowledge in the academic landscape.

Leadership Opportunities

Extolling the brilliance of Black minds entails shifting power dynamics in classrooms where Black minds are often disempowered. A key strategy for accomplishing this end is to provide Black boys and men with leadership opportunities. As noted by Wood and Harris III (2017a), "Provide them with opportunities to be 'center stage' in an environment where they are usually 'back stage'" (p. 58). Every classroom has a power structure. In many classrooms, the teacher or professor is the key power figure. In such classrooms, educators "stand and deliver" information to students who are eager to receive their knowledge. Friere (1970) referred to this type of instruction as "banking education," whereby educators "deposit" information into the hearts and minds of students. The work of critical scholars has long been vocal about the illegitimacy of this approach. These scholars argue that students have the ability to contribute to the learning environment. Whether the discourse is in early childhood or doctoral education, learners can contribute to the knowledge domain (Harper & Wood, 2015).

In other classrooms, the power structure is more democratic in nature. In these classes, educators share the "power" by giving students an opportunity to contribute. The range of what this looks like can be expansive, from simple opportunities to respond to queries in small and large groups to tangible opportunities for learners to lead in disseminating knowledge. For example, a high school teacher may upend the power dynamic in their classroom by allowing students to give part of the lecture, report on an aspect of the readings, or share their own perspectives where they occupy the position of power. Power dynamics in the classroom can also transcend direct instruction. In many elementary classrooms, formal and informal student leadership opportunities are provided. For example, these classes often have student leaders who assist the teacher, are responsible for holding others accountable, and serve as defacto representatives for their peers. Indeed, the range of power dynamics in a classroom can vary greatly.

To extol the brilliance of Black minds requires educators to afford opportunities for students to wield power in the classroom as described. Moreover, it requires that Black children, youth, and adults have access to this power in a manner that centers them as leaders in the classroom. This is critical because the classroom is a space where many Black boys and men feel disempowered. As noted by Harris III and Harper (2008), the vast majority of teachers in K-12 classrooms are White females. The pervasiveness of their presence shapes the power structure of classrooms as domains that are best suited for those who are White and those who identify as women. This is not to disparage White women, as many of these educators do an incredible job in supporting the learning, development, and success of Black boys and men. However, at some point, if a student does not see someone who looks like them in front of the classroom, the domain becomes situated as one that does not resonate with them. Students begin to disassociate from these environments, instead placing their time, energies, and interests in domains that connect to their being. Thus, it is not surprising that Harris III and Harper (2008) noted that, by middle school, many boys have started to disassociate with school. By this age, the boy who is studious, asks questions in class, and engages frequently with the teacher is often the same child who is picked on and bullied in the school yard. Similar challenges may emerge based on racial identities, and certainly the convergence of racial and gender identities serve to exponentiate this occurrence. The good news is that all educators have the power to change the power dynamics.

One key strategy for doing so is to provide Black boys and men with opportunities to serve as leaders on group projects, in small and large group discussions, in class debates and classroom senates, and in determining assignments and readings. In a previous study, we found that teachers who were nominated by their principals for having a documented record of success in teaching boys and young men of color regularly provided leadership opportunities. In that study, one teacher from California stated, "Providing leadership where students of color serve in leadership roles with projects [is essential]. They rise to the task at hand and do amazing work compared to when they are not in leadership roles" (Wood & Harris III, 2017b, p. 57). In fact, the exemplar teachers in this study noted that there are manifold benefits when boys of color are provided with opportunities to be leaders in learning spaces. These benefits included having greater confidence in their academic abilities, enhanced engagement in the learning environment, a greater sense of belonging in school, and a greater quality of work.

Conveying High Expectations

In the 1960s, a scholar named Nevitt Sanford (1962) offered a powerful theory on how to support the learning, development, and success of students. This theory, referred to as "challenge and support" has been a mainstay of student development curriculum since then. The theory suggests that there are two primary conditions for students to reach their highest level of potential. The first is that they must be challenged. This challenge requires them to be exposed to new ideas, concepts, and information that pushes them to learn. A rigorous curriculum is essential for students to develop their knowledge, skills, and dispositions to reach their maximum potential. Sanford also argued that students need to be supported. Support, as argued by Wood and Harris III (2017b), refers to the availability of assistance. Specifically, students need to know there is support available to them to reach the challenges set before them. Educators can be available to meet with students before, during, and after class. They must be willing to readily serve as resources for students. It is the combination of challenge and support that is purported to benefit student achievement.

As a caveat, Sanford argued that there must be a combination of challenge and support. For example, too much challenge and too little support may result in students becoming dismayed, dejected, and overwhelmed. In contrast, too much support and too little challenge fails to enable students to grow. Thus, there is an optimal balance between the concepts. As noted in previous works, this theory (like many of the theories in education) is useful as a starting point but has limitations with respect to underserved students of color. Specifically, my colleagues and I have argued (see Wood et al., 2015; Wood & Harris III, 2017a, 2017b) that the theory of challenge and support makes erroneous assumptions that two other necessary preconditions are already in place. For instance, an educator can challenge a student to the highest level of rigor possible, but if the student does not believe that the educator believes in their ability to reach the challenge set forth, they will never rise to the expectation.

As such, challenge must be met with high expectations. According to Wood et al. (2015), conveying high expectations occurs when students know educators believe in their ability to succeed. Said differently, no one has ever risen to low expectations. As such, high expectations are a critical precondition for students exposed to a rigorous curriculum. Similarly, support does not always translate to success either. An educator must make themselves available to provide support to students, host office hours, create opportunities for informal engagement with students, and the like; however, if a student does not believe that the educator truly cares about them and their success, then that support will go unused. Stated differently, authentic care is a precondition to the use of support. Therefore, it is the combination of these factors (e.g., challenge and support, high expectations, and authentic care) that is necessary to create the environment necessary for student success.

The aforementioned practices are merely a few examples of the many ways that educators can extol the brilliance of Black males in the classroom. Thus far, strategies for disrupting narratives of distrust (criminalization) and disregard (perceptions of academic inferiority) have been extended. In the next chapter, I examine similar strategies that can counteract pathologized perspectives of Black males. As informed by the D-Three effect, these perspectives communicate 'disdain' to Black males. These messages denigrate Black male learners, their families, and their communities.

Personal Story – When Your Teacher's a "G"

While Ms. Harrington was the worst teacher I have ever encountered, the next year God blessed me with one of the greatest teachers and men I have ever met—Mr. G. Mr. G. is a wonderful human being and a marvelously gifted teacher. He entered the classroom with relentless energy, humor, and passion. He loved teaching and made learning fun. We were taught to think outside-the-box, to embrace new ideas, and to embrace our imaginations. I vividly remember him playing on words such as "escargot" and watching the "S-Car go!", and learning what is sometimes described as the longest word in the English language pneumonoultramicroscopicsilicovolcanoconiosis, which is an extended spelling of silicosis (a type of lung disease). And, I also remember discussions about whether or not Mt. Everest is actually higher than K2 (Mt. Godwin-Austen). In his class, learning was not simply fun, but an adventure.

More importantly, Mr. G. recognized that I loved to write and was pretty good at it. He capitalized on this, nominating me for writer camps, allowing me to write and rewrite short stories, and pushing me to create my own voice in text. He empowered me to feel like I could be anyone that I wanted to be and excel in any field that I wanted to. He did not see me as a villain or a menace, but as his pupil and his mentee. The juxtaposition between fifth grade and sixth grade is so great that the only metaphor that does justice to my memories is that I was in darkness and he brought me into the light. Even to this day, I am still connected with him. I regularly exchange messages with him on social media and have on many occasions expressed my deep gratitude to him. I do not know if he truly understands the depth of the impact he had on me. He gave me two important gifts. The first gift was the love of learning (a fire rekindled) and the second was hope. Although several years later I would encounter teachers like Ms. Harrington, these gifts were so powerful that I was buffered from these events. This is how I learned that traits such as grit, resilience, and perseverance are not innate, but environmental.

A great teacher is one of the most powerful tools of a promising future. During high school, I was a good student and was highly involved. In particular, I was highly engaged in a student club called Future Business Leaders of America. It was a powerful experience and provided me with a platform to compete with others. My competition was public speaking, and I worked for months each year preparing my speech for competition. I was closely guided by Mr. Micheli. Mr. Micheli was the school's business teacher. We would meet every day, find a semiprivate location, and I would practice my speech. He would hear it several times a day for months, helping me to hone every aspect of it.

What I took most from Mr. Micheli is that he truly believed in me. He had the highest expectations possible for my performance, and he pushed me to reach those expectations. Every word, every mannerism, every argument was carefully and tediously constructed to maximize the most from the material. He encouraged me to pull into the speech quotes and ideas that resonated with me. I made civil rights a core component of my message and incorporated phraseology and quotes from Martin Luther King Jr. For years I dedicated myself to improving my speech, and for years he poured time, energy, attention, and belief into me. It felt like we were in the competition together—it was not simply me, but both of us.

The hard work paid off; during my senior year, I won the competition for the State of California. With the win, I was advanced on to the national competition to compete on a larger stage. During the national competition, Mr. Micheli watched all the other competitors to see how they would match up against me. He studied their delivery, looking for any last-minute pointers. Then, it was my turn. I got up and performed the very best I could. When I sat down, a sense of elation ran through me. I knew I was going to win. At the awards ceremony, we were both on pins and needles. We were both cautiously optimistic, but incredibly anxious. The awards were read off for all the competitions, and finally it came to public speaking.

The master of ceremony opened the list to begin reading. As he read, it was immediately apparent that I had not won, nor was I placed anywhere in the top 3 speakers. I watched as other students jumped with elation, celebrating their hard-earned accomplishments. I was heartbroken and beaten down. With incredible sadness, I looked over at Mr. Micheli. He looked at me and told me that he was happy with the job I had done. As he said this, I could see him holding back tears. He was as invested in the competition as I was. I knew from that moment, and the many other moments before it, that he authentically cared about me and my success.

CHAPTER 6

BLACK DIGNITY

The biggest obstacle facing Black boys is perception.
> – Vanessa McCullers, Education Chair,
> Moms of Black Boys United

It's important to educate and teach the truth to our children! There is no superior or inferior group.
> – Ilyasah Shabazz, Advocate and Daughter of
> Malcolm X and Dr. Betty Shabazz
> (Statement from Black Minds Matter)

Educators have been taught to believe that student success is a function of students' effort, grit, and engagement as opposed to the environments in which they are educated. These dominant perspectives are rooted in a rich educational tradition that places the onus of student success on students themselves, as opposed to the institutions and the personnel who educate them (Duckworth, 2016; Kuh, 2003). As a result, Black males often encounter a microaggression subtype referred to as *pathologizing culture*. As articulated by Sue et al. (2007), pathologizing culture refers to "the notion that the values and communication styles of the dominant/ White culture are ideal" (p. 276). Sue provides examples of microaggressions that pathologize culture, such as statements about stereotyping Black people as loud, angry, and having lowly values.

In my work with Frank Harris III, we have extended this concept to specifically focus on the perceived academic cultures of the dominant majority. Given the pervasive stereotypes about Black males in learning environments, they are often perceived through a lens that disdains them by blaming them, their families, and their communities for inadequate outcomes. This is only further exacerbated when there are poor dynamics between educators and the students they serve. There are numerous examples of statements that connote this notion, that the academic cultures of Black people, and Black males in general, are less than the dominant ideal.

As part of our research, we have collected narratives from teachers, interviewed professors, and conducted focus groups with noninstructional educators. A pervasive theme embedded in these conversations, even with those who may view themselves as being socially conscious, is to denigrate the values of Black males, as well as the homes, communities, and schools from which they emanate. Based on our experience in engaging educators, we see that the pathologized comments made about Black males are aggregated in seven primary areas. I provide an overview of these areas next along with representative statements often made by educators in these areas:

1. **Dismissal of passion for learning** (e.g., "they are lazy," "they don't care," "they are only here for the financial aid," "they aren't here for school, just for socializing");

2. **Being futureless** (e.g., "they don't see a future for themselves," "they have nothing to lose");

3. **Portrayed as troubled** (e.g., "they have too many problems," "they are troubled," "I'm a faculty member, not a social worker," "they have family drama");

4. **Parental apathy** (e.g., "their parents value sports over school," "their parents are not invested in their education," "their parents don't get involved");

5. **Vilification of parent communication** (e.g., "these parents are aggressive," "they are confrontational and loud," "they lack tact and candor");

6. **Denigration of family structures** (e.g., "they come from unstructured home environments," "they have fatherless homes," "they don't have good role models"); and

7. **Community deprecation** (e.g., "they come from bad communities," "they live in the hood or ghetto," "they are the outgrowth of generational poverty").

Almost assuredly, someone reading this volume who has engaged educators (in any capacity) will recognize these statements and perspectives as commonplace. Overall, these comments demonstrate a larger perspective where some educators see Black males through a deficit lens. Ultimately, these messages suggest that Black males face innumerable barriers to success. These barriers are often attributed to students, their families, and their communities. But, they can also be attributed to larger societal pressures that disadvantage them. The common tie is that Black people are pathologized with the underlying assumption that the barriers they face in school and life are insurmountable.

Essien and I have examined the myriad of pathologized messages that Black males receive, beginning in early childhood education. In her study of microaggressions experienced by the parents of Black children, she extended three patterns that face Black communities (Essien & Wood, 2018b). She noted that the parents of Black children are assumed to be low-income, to have fatherless homes, and to come from unstructured home environments. There were a number of experiences documented in her research that showed how these messages manifest in the earliest levels of education. For instance, numerous parents in her study noted that they were assumed to be low-income; these messages were communicated to them during home visits (e.g., statements about what they could afford), during school enrollment (e.g., being questioned about subsidy status), and in general statements about their neighborhoods (e.g., oh, you live *there* . . .). The assumption that Black boys emanate from low-income homes is a popular portrayal in the wider media (Clawson, 2002). Moreover, this assumption is sometimes communicated to the parents of Black children without thought to how it may be degrading and hurtful. I have experienced similar interactions with educators, have heard an educator recommend a critical reading resource to two Black parents and then say, "Well, it's a really critical resource, I don't know if *you* could afford it." Another example from my research with Essien was a parent who noted the following:

> It was hard leaving my son for his first day at the early childhood center, he dug his nails into my leg and held on for dear life screaming at the top of his lungs. My husband and our parents were his only babysitters and they all stood peering through the glass behind the door while Mommy did the "dirty deed." I begged, pleaded and bribed him to let go but he hadn't budged. Another parent, a mother, comes in and

drops her child off. The little girl walks in with a smile and runs of to play with the other children. With daring eyes the mother turns to me and says, "this is why it's so important for their dad to be in their lives." I used all four of my degrees to politely tear her . . . soul to pieces. (Essien & Wood, 2018b, slide 12).

As evident in this example, the assumption that Black men emanate from fatherless homes and are deadbeat dads is pervasive. One important point that was uncovered in this study was that these assumptions (at face value) may seem innocent and harmless. For instance, it is correct that Black children are more likely to be on free and reduced lunch than their peers (Wood & Harris III, 2017a) and raised in mother-only homes (Thistle, 2006). Of course, these perspectives do not take into account the erroneous assumptions that undergird this perspective, nor the effect of family destruction during slavery, the communalistic rearing that occurs within Black communities, or the criminal industrial complex that has systematically removed Black men from Black homes (McAdoo, 2007). Notwithstanding, we found that the messages and the contexts within which they were rendered communicated racial slights and insults to the parents who received them.

Even in cases where students came from low-income homes or did not have a father present, the messages were hurtful and dismissive. My research demonstrates that educators need to be critically aware of the ways in which they frame Black life and culture when speaking about people of color. It should be noted that many educators are fully unaware of how their deficit views of Black people cause harm; in fact, many of them have good intentions and want to uplift Black children. However, their ability to do so when their perspectives are so deeply informed by bias and stereotypes is inhibited. In other words, good intentions are not enough as the "road to hell is paved with good intentions."

Given this, a core component of Black Minds Pedagogy is to extol the dignity of Black males. This involves esteeming, honoring, and conveying respect for Black people and culture. Educators who extol the dignity of Black males see them through an asset-based lens that embraces and values Black male learners, their families, and their communities. Extolling the dignity of Black males, in and of itself, is an act of civil resistance, as this runs counter to dominant narratives about Black males. There are a number of practices that can be employed to connote this belief. Some of these practices include: (a) knowing students' names; (b) building intrusive relationships; (c) being fully present; (d) welcoming engagement; (e) connecting to people, not services; and (f) leveraging summative symbols. What these practices look like will be explored in more detail in the following sections.

Knowing Students' Names

The act of dignifying Black males begins with the simple practice of knowing students' names and referring to them by their name when engaging them. Engaging this practice is a method for communicating the dignity and inherent worth of Black minds. Unfortunately, ample research suggests that Black males are often not afforded the dignity of educators knowing their names. For example, Allen (2010) offered the following quote from a Black male student in middle school:

She doesn't know my name, just the other day we were having a test review game and like she was throwing popsicle sticks out of the [cup], and I'm like, you know, I'm the only Black kid in your class, uh, next to three other Black kids in there, and I'm like one of the most goofiest ones in there and so she pulls my name out and she goes D-Darrell? And it's her own handwriting and everything and I'm like, "Come on now, lady. I've been in your class now for about four months now and you don't know my names." She doesn't know me or anything like that. (p. 130)

While some educators may be aware of students' legal or "government" names, it is essential that educators take the time to learn the names by which students prefer to be referenced (I call these their referent names). These names should be used when referring to them, as this demonstrates the importance of and one's value for their presence. For instance, while my government name is Jonathan, I have gone by my middle name, Luke, my entire life. I am not responsive to Jonathan because I am so rarely referenced by this name. In a similar manner, educators should be attentive to the names that Black males prefer. Moreover, educators should also be attentive to the correct pronunciation of students' names. In some instances, educators may find that Black boys and young men have unique names that employ pronunciation with which they are not familiar. I believe that educators should be particularly attentive to these names, as they represent individuals who have traversed successive levels of education and often experienced those who did not care enough to refer to them by their preferred name. Moreover, referent names often have meaning associated with them, meaning that is derived from the name itself or those who bestowed the name upon them. As noted in other works, knowing students' names is "a powerful way of conveying that their presence and personhood is important" (Wood & Harris III, 2017a, p. 39).

It is common for educators, particularly those in postsecondary education, to contend that it is unrealistic for them to learn the names of all of their students. Often, this perspective is adjoined with conversations about excessive teaching loads and student enrollments. However, the response should not be to dismiss the practice, but to employ the practice in realistic ways. This is particularly common in higher education, where the faculty members' duration of engagement with the student is more limited. Despite this, learning students' names is an essential foundation for building relationships with them and supporting their success.

My colleagues and I recommend employing a triage approach, where educators begin learning the names of students who emanate from groups that have historically experienced disproportionate impact (underperformance compared to other groups). By beginning with these students, educators will likely prioritize student groups that are often not prioritized in educational settings. Then, after learning these names, educators can begin learning the names of other students in their classrooms. In discussing this topic during a training in Michigan, one faculty member provided the following comments:

> Educators constantly challenge students to learn information that they may struggle with. Teachers speak with an argot of academic lingo specific to their discipline, communicate new concepts and theories, and constantly require students

to push themselves in their learning and development. Any educator who downplays the importance of saying a student's name correctly does so from a standpoint of privilege that their students rarely have. (Harvell, 2016, as cited in Wood & Harris III, 2017b, p. 39)

As evidenced in this quote, educators are asking students to learn difficult concepts, new ideas, and to constantly "go beyond" what they believe they have the capacity to learn. In return, educators should have a commitment to doing the same thing by emulating the dispositions that seek to foster. The first and most important aspect of this practice is to learn students' names.

Intrusive Relationships

Another strategy for demonstrating the inherent dignity of Black minds is to be intrusive in building relationships with students. According to Wood et al. (2015), this involves proactively engaging relationships with students as a pathway for fostering an enhanced ability to support their learning and development. Intrusive relationships demonstrate the value (i.e., inherent dignity) of Black minds by prioritizing engagement with them. This, of course, is particularly powerful for Black males who are rarely "centered" in learning environments. My research (see Wood, 2014) has focused on how practices occur in the classroom that decenter Black males from the learning experience. For example, many Black males have reported that their faculty members employ an "approach me first" or "prove yourself first" stance. This stance involves educators restricting their engagement (through investment of time with students) until after the student has demonstrated their dedication to the class by approaching the faculty member, performing well, and being engaged in class discussion. However, given that many boys and young men of color are apprehensive about engaging in the classroom for fear of reifying stereotypes about their academic abilities, the two groups (educators and students) rarely meet in the middle. The outgrowth is that Black boys and young men are ignored in educational settings.

Beyond this, being intrusive about establishing relationships with students is essential, given that many boys (in general) and boys of color (in particular) are socialized to be apprehensive about seeking help. For some males, having to ask for help is associated with being weak or inferior. This runs counter to male gender socialization where boys are taught that, to be a man, they need to imbue confidence and a sense of control (Harris III & Harper, 2008). Thus, for some Black boys, having to seek help from faculty, go to tutoring services, or use resources at their schools or colleges can conflict with their identities as men. As such, boys and men who may be apprehensive about their abilities may be more reluctant to engage in relationships with educators. This can be a function of their concern that educators may not want to engage them, and this can simultaneously be affected by students' concerns that greater connections with educators may produce circumstances that will illuminate areas where their abilities are lacking.

There are many strategies that educators can employ to build intrusive relationships with students. Like knowing students' names, these involve simple strategies. For example, one strategy includes learning about students with interest. This involves taking the time as an educator to learn about students' academic, career, and life goals. It can also include learning personal information about them and their families. With this information, educators can more readily build personal relationships with students and demonstrate their authentic care for students personal and familial success. Moreover, when educators are learning this information, they should convey their interest through active learning (e.g., shaking their head, nodding, verbal affirmations) to demonstrate they are truly interested in what they are learning. Learning about students can certainly take place in the classroom; however, this can occur more readily out-of-class. Out-of-class engagement is often where relationships are built because this provides a greater opportunity to learn about students and have discussions that are not necessarily centered on academics.

Another strategy for building intrusive relationships is to proactively check in with students to see how they are doing. These unprompted conversations, both during and after class, can demonstrate that educators value Black male learners. Proactively checking in with students can also be useful for identifying issues that may lead to physical or emotional withdrawal from a classroom before they occur. Many educators, particularly those in postsecondary education, may have experiences with students where, partway through a semester, a student simply disappears. This occurs often due to unwelcoming environments within school settings that are further complicated by challenges outside of the classroom. By checking in with students, educators can more adeptly identify issues before they occur.

Fully Present

Like all other professionals, educators have numerous responsibilities that compete for their time. This can include preparing for class, meeting with students and parents, attending faculty meetings, preparing organizational assessments, and the like. Beyond this, educators also have issues that may arise in their personal lives that can also impede upon their time. As such, it can be very difficult for educators to be fully focused when engaging in conversations with students. The result of this can occur when educators are talking with students but are seemingly distracted, inattentive, or multitasking at the same time. Obviously, such practices do not demonstrate the inherent dignity and worth of Black males.

Building a personal relationship with students involves being fully present. Specifically, this entails maintaining one's attention on Black males when engaged with them in one-on-one interactions. This communicates respect for their presence. There is often a paradox in the experience of Black males in schools, where they feel they are being hypersurveilled, yet also invisible at the same time. Being fully present helps to address the latter concern given that Black males often experience school and college as isolating. As stated by Wood and Harris III (2017a), "Students who often feel invisible and unimportant" need to be "seen" and "valued" by educators. As such, it is essential that the interactions they have with educators demonstrate the exact opposite message. Therefore, being fully present when engaging Black males in conversation is critical. With this in mind, it may be more beneficial for educators to be fully present for shorter conversations than to have longer periods of engagement that are marked by a lack of full presence. Stated differently, it is better to be fully present for 5 minutes than be distracted while engaging Black males for 10 minutes.

Welcoming Engagement

Across the nation, many schools, colleges, and universities measure the extent to which students are engaged. A litany of different surveys has been created to determine the frequency to which students ask and respond to questions in class and participate in group discussions. These data are then used to make statements about the engagement, or lack thereof, of certain student groups. It is often the case that these surveys show that Black males are less engaged than their peers. The resulting perception is that Black males do not care about school, are lazy, and are not focused. While measuring the extent that students are engaged is an important action, this does not provide insight on why some students are more or less engaged.

When considering the educational experiences of students of color, these surveys and the resultant sensemaking miss the mark, because they fail to ask a simple question: Did our Black males ever feel welcome to engage? It is not simply enough for educators to provide opportunities for students to engage in the classroom. A Black Minds Pedagogy is one that intentionally demonstrates that students' engagement is both invited and desired. Instead of focusing on engagement, educators should be more concerned with whether or not students felt welcome to engage.

In my center's research on this topic, we have routinely found that feeling welcome to engage with educators (both inside and outside the classroom) is one of the top predictors of Black male development and success. Bearing this in mind, educators have a responsibility to foster an environment where students feel welcome to engage. This involves actions that communicate that their perspectives, presence, experiences, and minds are valued. Simple statements conveyed with authenticity can foster a welcoming environment for Black boys and men. Some of these statements may include: "I'm really looking forward to your comments on today's topic because you have so much to offer," "I'm glad you are here—the class didn't feel the same when you were gone last week," and "When you shared that remark yesterday, it really hit home for me, I'm learning so much from you."

Outside the classroom, a welcoming environment can be fostered through a number of strategies that involve simple meaningful exchanges. This can include smiling at students, waving at them, saying hello, talking with them about academic matters, having discussions about nonacademic matters, and offering support and assistance. These exchanges demonstrate that Black minds have value in an educational system that systematically communicates the opposite message. Indeed, this is an act of civil resistance, as it fosters a new environment that runs counter to the pervasive dismissal of Black male presence in educational settings.

Connecting Students to People, Not Services

In our 2015 study, my colleagues and I found that educators who had a proven record of success in teaching men of color in community colleges often employed a practice called connecting students to people, not services (see Wood et al., 2015). This practice involves making meaningful connections for students with other educators, rather than simply referring them to available resources. For example, let's say a student is meeting with an educator and the educator learns that the student is in need of financial assistance. Rather than simply referring the student to financial aid, the educators in the study directly connected students to people they knew and trusted. This practice is rooted in the notion that there are some educational professionals who simply do not care and will not prioritize Black males. Thus, when making referrals, educators were careful to restrict their recommendations to people they knew and trusted. They wanted to ensure students would be engaging with other educators who would care about them in similar ways.

This is an important practice for several reasons. First, educators who effectively work with boys and men of color have made ardent steps to build relationships typified by trust, mutual respect, and authentic care. These educators are careful not to make referrals unless they were certain that Black males would engage with other professionals who were similarly committed to their success. Otherwise, the trust they have built with a student could be jeopardized, especially if their advice resulted in adverse interactions with others. Second, as previously noted, many Black boys and men may be apprehensive about seeking out help. As such, this practice was employed as a strategy for reducing instances of help-seeking. Specifically, the educators in our study referred students for help by making direct connections in a manner that ensured the connections were actually made. This could involve an educator talking with another colleague on the phone with the student present, explaining the issues that were occurring, and letting them know that the student was on his way and that colleague needed to be there to welcome him. In many cases, it actually involved physically walking students to the office to which they were being referred. This practice demonstrates a deep sense of commitment to students who often felt that educators could "care less" about them and their futures.

Third, this practice can also serve to ensure that students are actually getting the support they need. On many college and university campuses, there is a plethora of resources and services that can help students address a multitude of needs. These services often include career counseling, transfer services, tutoring, computer labs, the library, financial aid, academic advisors, and many other services. However, these services are only beneficial to the extent that they are used by Black males and help to address the challenges students face. Connecting students with people, not services, increases the likelihood that their experience will result in the support necessary for them to address problems as they arise, and in some cases, before they arise. Fourth, this practice also works to extend students' networks to include other educators who similarly care about their success. For example, a classroom teacher who refers a student to a close colleague in financial aid has now created an opportunity for an additional relationship that can be beneficial to the student. If the colleague in financial aid then turns around and connects the student with a colleague in academic advising, the student now has three educators who they know are truly committed to their success. As such, this is an essential practice for communicating the inherent dignity of Black minds.

Utilizing Summative Symbols

One strategy for demonstrating an educator's investment in Black males is to utilize summative symbols as a source of motivation. Summative symbols refer to symbols that demonstrate care and connection between the educator and the student. In the context of our work with men of color, these symbols included material items that were often limited in monetary value but held a deep sense of meaning between them. In all cases when we have seen this practice employed, the symbols served as a source of motivation for the students to work harder, reach their goals, and be resilient in the face of obstacles.

One example of this emerged in a study my colleague Frank Harris III led that focused on the narratives of men of color who successfully transferred from a community college to a 4-year institution. In that study, a student named Ryan noted how he nearly dropped out of college. Ryan was having trouble getting his financial aid monies, and as a result, was unable to purchase the book for his class. After several class sessions and continued struggles with financial aid, Ryan had become dismayed. During the class, he made the decision that he was done with college and was going to drop out. His faculty member, a White female, noticed that Ryan was seemingly less engaged than normal. After the class session ended, she made the intentional effort to connect with Ryan before he left (a decision that ultimately changed his future). She asked Ryan what was wrong, and he explained his challenge with getting access to the course text. This is what occurred:

> She saw that I couldn't get the textbook, so she gave me [hers]. I was just like, man this is amazing, for her to do that for me, it just showed she really cares. And I tried to give it back to her at the end of the semester, like "thank you." And she wouldn't take it, she said "keep the book." She said, "If you want, then you can pay it forward," but I needed the book so much, it was helping me how to write, teaching me how to cite, and grammar that I kept the book as a reference. And, I still have it . . . I keep it in my room where I study, I see it

Black Minds Matter

every day, and I keep it there to use it, but always because it motivates me, it reminds me of when I almost quit and how she helped me when she didn't have too.

The book served as a summative symbol of her commitment to Ryan and his success. Ultimately, Ryan retained the book as a reference but also as a source of motivation to reach his goals. Another example of this emerged from one of my earlier studies on Black men in community colleges. The study focused on academic success and involved interviews with a number of Black males attending a college located in Arizona. In that study, one student named Lawrence was talking about his future goals. I had asked Lawrence to discuss what he saw himself doing as a career in the future. As part of this description of his future goals, he noted how a high school educator had given him a summative symbol that served as a source of motivation to achieve his goals. Lawrence stated:

Where do I see myself 10 years from now? Honestly, I mean I can't really tell what the future holds, you know. But, I want to see myself in somebody's restaurant cooking some great dishes for people to eat. You know, people telling me, "yeah, you cook real good." Me wearing my chef coat-that's what I really want to do. I just want to wear my chef coat. I mean, honestly, I mean the only thing I really just hope for right now is just getting to wear my chef coat. I have a chef coat at home sitting [in] my closest, sitting there collecting dust. My high school teacher gave it to me . . . I have this little jacket in my closet, and I just really want to wear that "cause once I

144

wear that, once I have that on and I'm in someone's kitchen and I have that on, then I can actually tell myself I made it." (Wood, Hilton, & Hicks, 2014, p. 55)

In this case, the gift of a chef's coat served to inspire Lawrence. When he spoke about the coat, he was visibly emotional, which further emphasized the importance of this symbol to him. It should be noted that Lawrence was a student who was in special education and had reported being moved from classroom to classroom by educators. His counselor had decided to place him in a culinary class as a last-ditch effort, as Lawrence was already dismayed with school. That decision transformed his life, leading to a commitment to pursue further studies at his local community college. As such, this summative symbol and the interactions with the educator who gave it to him helped Lawrence see school as worthwhile and to feel a sense of belonging in school, a feeling that had evaded him in school prior to that point.

In totality, the sensemaking and practices recommended here and in the previous chapters provide a framework for enacting Black Minds Pedagogy in schools, colleges, and universities. Ultimately, this pedagogy is designed to enhance the success of Black boys and men by countering the pervasive ways they are stereotyped in school. In the final chapter, I emphasize the role that love has within the process of employing Black Minds Pedagogy.

Personal Story – Otherfathering

During college, my father became incarcerated. Given that he was the primary breadwinner for our family, I struggled trying to stay afloat financially. No longer could I call home if I was in desperate need of support—I had to figure it out on my own. For two years, I struggled financially and lived on a very limited income. My twin brother and I both struggled with a place to stay. Fortunately, we were both involved in student government, so he would often sleep in his office when he did not have a home. Similarly, I vacillated between sleeping in my car, my brother's garage, and with friends. While housing was a concern, it was not as pressing of a concern for me as food. On many occasions, I found myself without money to pay for food. There were many times when I went two or three days without eating. When things became really desperate, I would scrounge change off of the ground to get food. I did so because, at that time, you could get a bean burrito and a cup of water for less than a dollar from Taco Bell. If there were student events, I would often attend because of the free food. In fact, my attendance would often determine whether or not I ate at all.

During this time, I met a local youth pastor and campus paraeducator named Mr. Andal. Andal was quiet, welcoming, and an incredibly powerful Black leader. He was concerned with students' spiritual growth, but he was also concerned with ensuring that people were stable. He was aware of my situation and a number of other students who suffered from the same challenges. Once I finally got a stable place to live, he would come by and drop off a box of healthy food. It would include canned goods, fresh fruits, and other items. Like most men, I was incredibly reluctant to ask for help, and being provided with a food box was humbling and made me feel inferior. So, when Andal would come by, I would always tell him that I did not need the box and that he should save it for someone who really needed the food. Regardless of what I said, he would insist that I take the box, noting that if I did not need it, I might know of others who would. In reality, we both knew it was for me. When he would leave, my austere of pride would drop. I would begin rummaging through the box immediately to see what I could eat. Andal knew he had to be intrusive with support while letting me retain my dignity. He knew that I needed the support, and he would not let me refuse the help that was needed.

Andal is an example of someone who conveys value and respect to students. While Andal served as a spiritual guide and system of support, my interactions with another man, Dr. Kant, further demonstrated the role that otherfathering can have on a student. Otherfathering, like othermothering, occurs when Black men serve as advocates and father-like figures for Black men who are not their sons for the purpose of transforming and uplifting them (Bridges, 2011). Some time, during my freshman year, I was walking on campus, and a Black male professor saw me. His name was Dr. Kant and he was known as an incredible leader on the campus, in the state, and in the nation for Black faculty issues and faculty rights. When Dr. Kant saw me, he introduced himself saying, "Hello, Black man." He approached me, struck up a conversation, and demonstrated that he was there, along with other Black faculty and staff, to support my success. Every time I saw him, he acknowledged my presence, stopped to talk with me, truly demonstrated a care for me and my success, and did anything he could to support me.

Dr. Kant occupies a unique space in my life. He is my mentor, but he has always been more than that; he has been a father-like figure to me. Here is the unique aspect of our relationship: I never took a single class with Dr. Kant. In fact, I avoided his classes because I was worried that I would let him down by not meeting his expectations. Regardless, we grew close because I knew I could always trust him, that he always had my best interests at heart, and that he was not going to take any excuses. He is a walking example of how educators can have a meaningful impact on all students, and that there is a responsibility to do so, even if they are not enrolled in their own courses. Taking a few minutes out of his day one time to talk with me set me on a different path and created a lifelong relationship.

I have acknowledged Dr. Kant extensively in my work. Many of the books I have written have been dedicated to him, a small level of appreciation for an immense influence. While I had not seen Dr. Kant since my undergraduate years, I did have the pleasure of engaging him recently at a conference. Knowing that I was going to see him was exciting, but foremost was that I wanted him to know I am still and will always be dedicated to the community, that I was someone who would always stand up and advocate for our people, that I had served as a mentor and positive role model to others, and that I had invested in others as much as he had invested his time, energies, and efforts in me. When I saw him, it was like time had not passed at all. We talked about our families, our trips to the homeland (Africa), and our current areas of advocacy.

As the conversation drew to an end, I said to him:

I just want to take a moment to tell you something. I don't know if you truly know the influence and impact that you have had on my life. When I was coming here, I told a close friend that you were my mentor, but I also told him that you were much more than that. As you know, my father was imprisoned, and while I did not have him for an important part of my life, I knew that I could look to you for guidance, advice, and support. I have always considered you like a father—you are far more than a mentor, you have been like a father.

Without delay, he leaned forward and said to me, "Luke, I have always viewed you as a son, you are my son." This is not an exchange between two Black men that is commonly discussed. I have been blessed to have critical male and female role models who were dedicated to my success, who served as otherfathers and othermothers.

All names used here are pseudonyms.

CHAPTER 7

EMBEDDING LOVE IN EDUCATION

This volume has sought to demonstrate that there is a need to extol the brilliance, dignity, and morality of Black minds. I have argued that doing so is an act of civil resistance by demonstrating love to a population from which this virtue has been withheld. Early in my career, I was introduced to the writings of the now-late Asa Hilliard. Hilliard was a Pan Africanist and a leading educational researcher who wrote extensively across fields, with a particular focus on Afrocentric teaching principles and practices. Among his many quotes that have resonated with me is the following assertion about children:

I have never encountered any children in any group who are not geniuses. There is no mystery on how to teach them. The first thing you do is treat them like human beings and the second thing you do is love them.

– Asa Hilliard

As a person of faith, I have always been taught that we are to love our neighbors as ourselves. My Christian tradition has told us to treat other people how we would like to be treated as a method for fostering a better world. As an educator, we have the privilege of not only teaching our neighbors, but the children of our neighbors as well. Given this, and informed by Dr. Hilliard's perspective, I offer following:

Love your neighbor as yourself and love their children as your children. Teach them with love, discipline them with love, build personal relationships with love, as if they were your own.

In theory, most educators would agree with this notion. They would argue that they love their students and want the very best for them. However, Black males are often dehumanized in society, so the love that is extended to them is not the same type of love that may be extended to other children, as they are not viewed in the same manner. As a dehumanized group, the love extended to Black males is more theoretical than actual, more symbolic than real.

Informed by this perspective, I believe it is essential to address how love can be manifested in education. This is especially necessary for Black male students who may encounter educators who may not readily demonstrate that they are loved and cared about. For many educators, they may struggle to comprehend what a loving relationship may look like with Black males because too few actually carry out such relationships in actuality. Given this, it is prudent to consider what a loving relationship with Black males can look like. In doing so, I use my positionality as a parent of three beautiful Black children to translate what it means to love students as if they were our own. What follows are 10 points on what a practice of love can look like in the educational experience of Black boys and young men.

> **Ten Principles for Imbedding Love in Education with Black Males**
> 1. Excitement for arrival
> 2. Learn about them with interest
> 3. Want the best for them
> 4. Advocate for them
> 5. Guard them from others
> 6. Worry about them
> 7. Discipline them with love
> 8. Boast about them
> 9. Time investment
> 10. Shared investment

Excitement for Arrival

When my wife was pregnant with our son, there was an incredible sense of anticipation. We were excited about his impending arrival. Numerous thoughts, questions, and feelings ran through our minds. We wondered what he would look like, how it would feel to hold him, whose dispositions he would mirror, and whether or not we were truly ready to give him all that he needed. We went out and bought new furniture for his room, painted the walls, bought diapers, wipes, and powder. Our minds were fully engulfed with the excitement of his arrival, and we worked arduously to be prepared for the moment. As the time of his arrival grew closer, we began to consider what routes we would take: we did a test drive to the hospital, made sure to say in contact even more regularly than before, and discussed every conceivable decision we would make. When the baby finally arrived, there was an incredible sense of joy, pride, and emotion. We could not wait to show the baby to our friends, family, and extended network of colleagues. There was an excitement and an unmeasurable sense of pride about the ability to present him to the world.

Similarly, educators who truly love Black males will have an authentic sense of excitement about their arrival to school. In preparation for their arrival, educators will prepare their classrooms with great anticipation, considering every aspect of the class design (e.g., the images on the wall, the arrangement of the desks, the lighting in the room) and instructional delivery (e.g., the curriculum they will employ, the examples they will provide, the class projects they assign). On the first day of school, they will be full of anticipation, expressing their excitement without restriction for the presence of the beautiful and capable Black minds in their classrooms. This excitement will be conveyed so that students know their presence is valued. Upon arrival, educators must convey a deep sense of pride and joy in welcoming their new students, looking for every opportunity to tell others (particularly their fellow educators) about the wonderful gift of their presence.

Learn About Them With Interest

As with all my children, when my son was born, I was excited and intrigued about the notion of becoming a father. More importantly, I embraced every opportunity to learn about him. Like many other parents, I studied his every action. I tried my very best to understand what made him happy and sad, what made him laugh and cry, what comforted him, and what made him uneasy. As he got older, these curiosities evolved. For example, when he was learning to walk, I was excited about all of the smaller events leading up to that moment. I watched him crawl, then scoot, then attempt steps (and fall), then walk holding a table, and finally, take his first few steps unassisted. Every aspect of this process was new, interesting, and exciting. Overall, I studied him because I wanted to learn as much as I could about him with interest.

Similarly, educators who love Black minds will also welcome opportunities to study their students. They will learn about them with interest, trying to understand what makes them unique. They will engage questions such as: What are his likes and dislikes? How does he learn best? What is he interested in? What are the things that are important to him? What makes him unique? What are his family dynamics? What are central aspects of his culture? It is these types of questions that are necessary for truly learning about our students with interest. We must study them with the same degree of fervor that we would if they were our own children. In an educational setting, classroom educators are responsible for guiding learners just as parents are responsible for doing so at home. You cannot guide someone who you do not know.

Want the Best for Them

As a parent, I want the best for my children. I pray they will have fulfilling and meaningful lives. I hope that my children will enter into a world that allows them to create a better future for themselves, and eventually for their own families. In terms of careers, I want them to have careers that allow them to exercise their creativity, that provide them with opportunities to advance, and that continue the stability in their lives that my wife and I have worked so hard to create for them. I have often jokingly told my children,

"You can be whatever you want to be when you grow up—either a doctor or a lawyer." In reality, my comments are not meant to limit their goals to fields that are often considered prestigious, but to push them to work as hard as they can for whatever goals they have.

In a similar fashion, educators should want the very best for their students. This goes beyond the theoretical hope that they have "good" lives to a deeper investment of wanting the best for them as they would want for their own children. More specifically, this is not solely limited to their academic futures, but is inclusive of their personal and career goals. For younger children, these goals are unknown, so our goal is to create conditions that allow them to reach not-yet-known goals and dreams. For high school and college students, this involves wanting them to experience success organized around emerging and stated goals. Educators must want the best for their students; this is a central avenue for demonstrating love.

Advocate for Them

As a father of a Black son, I recognize that he lives in a world that was never designed for him. A world that ubiquitously perceives him through the lens of distrust, disdain, and disregard. Simply wanting the best for our students, in and of itself, is not enough. Therefore, I recognize that my love for him must be met with action. I advocate for my son to the best degree I know how. If I feel he is being mistreated, I speak out. If I see an opportunity for him, I secure it. Wanting the best for him means I am his advocate, because I truly desire to see him do well. To love Black minds, one must be an advocate for them.

This goes beyond one's own practice, as described throughout this book. This involves serving as an advocate for Black boys and men within educational institutions that routinely mar their dreams, inhibit their opportunities, and render them without support. Educators must be on-the-ground advocates for Black males. If they see school officials or other educators treating them in ways they would not like their own children to be treated, they must advocate for a different future. If they become aware of a program or resource that would benefit them, they must advocate for them to have access to it. If they learn about an impending opportunity that might benefit the student, they must politic for and position the student to gain that opportunity. Being an advocate requires care that is demonstrated through one's actions.

Guard Them From Others

Connected to the notion of being an advocate for Black males is the practice of guarding them from others. I have recognized, on some occasions, that certain individuals do not have the best interests of my children at heart. Even as someone who is well versed in issues facing Black children in education, I too have experienced challenges in helping my children navigate around certain educators who (I feel) have sought to harm their futures. As a parent, when this has occurred, my instinctual response was to step in and protect my children. In some cases, my children were never aware of what was taking place, because I simply handled issues I hoped they would never learn about. In other cases, the issue was clear and transparent to them, and thus, so were my efforts to guard them.

Black boys and young men are in need of guarding, likely even more than other children. In particular, this is due to the universal distrust of them. As a result, some educators are predisposed to surveilling them, targeting them, and seeking to destroy their dreams.

157

This is certainly a fact of life for Black males. Therefore, an educator who loves Black minds will guard them against others who would seek their destruction. In some cases, this will involve subtle actions that quietly guide and protect students without them being aware they are being guarded. For example, this could be as simple as referring a student to a specific service, framing their capacities differently in front of other colleagues, or providing them with an opportunity that simultaneously separates them from others who may have bad motives. In other cases, Black males will be acutely aware they are being targeted, and the guarding will be a clear demonstration of love and commitment for them and their success.

Worry About Them

I constantly worry about my children. I am concerned about their safety, their emotional well-being, their academic success, their friendships, and whether or not I am properly preparing them for the world. Moreover, I worry that they will struggle, that they will have opportunities stripped from them, and that they will encounter those who seek to tear them down. I worry about their interactions with people in positions of authority, such as teachers, law enforcement, and employers who may not care about them in the ways I do. Will these individuals build them up or tear them down? I constantly worry—I worry because I am invested in their success, and I do not want something to occur that I could have prevented, something that might inhibit them from living wonderful lives. Worrying is essential, because it allows parents to be better advocates for their children. It keeps them sharp and aware of impending issues, and it provides a pathway for proactively addressing issues when they arise and before they arise. Guided by my faith, my worries result in continuous thoughts and prayers for my children's welfare.

Similarly, when educators' love Black minds, they will worry about them with the same degree of intensity. They will worry about whether or not they understand the material. They will worry about their physical, social, emotional, and cognitive development. They will be consumed with knowing whether they are providing the learner with exactly what they need to be successful. Beyond the academic realm, they will be concerned about their futures. They will consider barriers that may emerge in their paths and proactively consider strategies for thwarting those barriers. In true parental fashion, they will communicate their concerns with loving determination in a manner that allows the student to know they are cared for. When students feel they are cared for, they are more likely to trust those who are imbuing this care.

Discipline Them With Love

Loving my children also carries with it a responsibility to ensure they are disciplined. Disciplining my children may be one of the most difficult responsibilities I have as a parent. I derive no pleasure from having to set and maintain boundaries for their words, dispositions, and actions. But, I do so because I know it is an essential aspect of raising productive citizens. That being said, when I discipline my children, my goal is to teach them the right way to handle difficult circumstances and to build them up. Thus, I discipline them with love and a focus on their personal edification.

In contrast, it is not uncommon for educators to discipline children with the goal of punishment, not edification. This is due to the widespread dehumanization of Black males that sees them as undeserving of nurturing and protection and as having malintent. For some educators, disciplining Black boys is a pathway for destroying them, bringing them down, and for controlling their actions and efforts. This is why Black males are overrepresented among students who are suspended and expelled. An educator who loves Black minds will seek to discipline (when necessary) for the purpose of building up, not tearing down. Sometimes there is a need to step in and provide corrective action, to offer honest feedback, and to critique. But, this should be done from a standpoint of love, with the goal of elevating them. This is conveyed through a demonstration of trust, mutual respect, and authentic care.

Boast About Them

Like other parents, I think my children are simply amazing. As such, those who know me well know that I speak about them often. In fact, there is rarely a course session or speech where I do not mention my children. I often have pictures on hand and videos of school plays that are readily cued to show others. In addition, I gain excitement in sharing stories about their new hobbies, activities, and interests. I do so because I am proud of them and want others to know too. Moreover, my comments paint a larger narrative about my children to others who do not know them in the same way I do.

In many ways, educators should have a similar disposition and perspective of Black males. They should see all their assets and be vocal for the purpose of ensuring that others are well aware of these assets, just as they would if they were their own. This practice is essential for fostering a counternarrative about Black males that portrays them as worthwhile. In fact, this notion was discussed in the chapter on Black dignity. Unfortunately, the pervasive deficit notions of Black males depict them as being lazy, uncaring about school, and attending school for nonacademic reasons (e.g., social life, sports). Therefore, boasting about them presents a counternarrative that is in direct conflict with the dominant narrative about this population.

Time Investment

Being a full-time educator, a diversity trainer, a business owner, a writer, a husband, and a father means that time for any aspect of my life is limited. However, as a parent, the most sacred part of our time is that which is spent with our children. As such, I spend every moment I can with my children (e.g., getting ready in the morning, family dinner nights, weekend bowling, sports practices and games). Even when I am out of town, I call home to speak with them, because I know our time is important. My investment of time in my children is a tangible way of demonstrating that I love them and care for them. By no means am I perfect; like all professionals, I struggle to balance work, life, and family, and I often will sacrifice sleep and my personal well-being to ensure that each area is adequately engaged.

As with the time we invest in our children, those who love Black minds will craft time out of their workdays to ensure they have demonstrated a time investment to their Black boys and men. One way of assessing the degree to which this is true is for educators to reflect on the students with whom they spent the most time positively engaging. Are these learner's Black males? If so, are Black males as represented among these learners as other students? This is important, because one cannot argue that they love their students (and their Black males in particular), yet not actually set aside time to engage with them. As noted, time investment is a demonstration of love. Moreover, personal relationships cannot only be built in the classroom. In fact, they are more likely to be created outside of the classroom during informal interactions where engagement is not compensatory (i.e., in the school yard, the hallways, during recess, breaks in between classes).

Shared Investment

I have a shared investment with my children. A shared investment is a manifestation of authentic care. It is the notion that our destinies, livelihoods, and cares are intertwined. I am invested in their success to the extent that, when they do well (e.g., achieve a strong grade, develop a new friendship, persist in the face of obstacles), I personally feel I have done well. In a like manner, if they do not do well (e.g., they miss the mark, experience conflict), I personally feel I have not done well. Their success is my success, and their failure is my failure. Maybe this is more a sense of responsibility with my son, since we share the same name, but it is also a more general responsibility that I hold as a parent.

In the same way, educators should also have a shared (or linked) investment with their students. When their students do well (e.g., they achieve, get a good grade, pass a tough test, demonstrate growth), an educator who holds an authentic care for them will personally feel as though they have done well. If they stumble, fall, or miss the mark (e.g., experience learning setbacks, are reprimanded, fail on an exam), the same educator will also feel as though they have not done well. This shared investment that parents hold with their children represents the same link that teachers can, and should, hold for their students. This notion is rooted in the traditions of collectivity and communalism, core aspects of the cultural traditions of communities of color.

Conclusion

In all, this chapter has set out to demonstrate that simple actions can be taken to demonstrate love. However, while simple, these actions will likely be very foreign in application to Black males for educators who have been socialized throughout their lives to see them through the lens of distrust, disdain, and disregard. As a caution, the translation between parenting and love and education should never be associated with infantilizing Black males. Infantilizing refers to perceptions of Black males that see them as babyish or younger than they actually are. Instead, it is better to apply the 10 aforementioned principles in a developmentally appropriate manner depending upon the age and grade level of the learner. Thus, the enactment of these principles will likely look very different in early childhood education than it will in doctoral education. With that in mind, embedding love into a system of injustice is an act of civil resistance. This act is essential for uplifting the voices, lives, and minds of Black males in education.

Personal Story – Finding Me

Loving our Black boys and young men is an essential component of a teaching practice that seeks to extol their brilliance, dignity, and morality. This is especially important given the innumerable pressures and challenges facing this population. As with any student group, life pressures can occur that influence their ability to engage and succeed in school. However, for Black males, the presence of campus agents who can validate and demonstrate their love to them in the midst of these challenges are often not present in the same way that it is for other students. I was fortunate that during my undergraduate years, I had professors who cared about me and my success. While their care was essential during all aspects of my educational experience, there were times when I faced greater challenges in my life that often inhibited my focus in school. The following is an example of one set of experiences that I was navigating while trying to traverse the collegiate environment. Fortunately, during this period of time, I was able to connect with educators who invested their time in helping me make sense of my experiences, affirmed my worth, and demonstrated that they cared about my welfare in general, not just my academic success.

For years I had searched for my mother. I knew her name, but not much more than that. I searched public databases, social media, and even used the small monies I had made from my internship to pay for address searches through a records company. All of this to no avail, I was never able to find her. I heard through another person I knew who had also been in foster care and adopted that they had used a private detective to find their family. It sounded like a good idea but far outside my financial resources. So, I dismissed the idea.

Then, one day I called the state of California adoptions department to gain clarification on a letter that they had sent me with non-identifiable information on my mother. During the discussion, the administrator I spoke with suggested that I consider hiring a private detective. I told them I would love to but I was concerned about the cost. They mentioned that they knew of one person who would often give reduced rates because they were more interested in uniting families than making money. I sent her an email that same day. The following day, she called me and asked for all the details I knew about my adoption and birth mother. I didn't have much to offer other than a name and a few cities she had lived in. She said she would call be back in a week or two. The next day I awoke up to an email, saying that she was able to find Joann and gave me her address. She told me that she was not in good shape, so to be prepared.

My entire life I had a felt a sense of rejection, knowing that I had been given away. I could not imagine how any mother could give away their own child. This is not to say that my upbringing was lacking, in fact the opposite. I grew up in a family where I was loved, cared for, and believed in. I had a wonderful upbringing, regardless of the racial dynamics I encountered. I already had a mother, I didn't need Joann, but I did want an understanding. Despite this, the notion of being rejected accompanied with the challenges of a transracial adoption was everpresent. Within a week, I made my way to try and find her. Fortunately, the address I had was only an hour and half away from my home. I asked a friend to come with me. We made the short trek into San Francisco, and then into the tenderloin district near the homeless shelters. As we got closer and closer, we found an apartment building that was incredible dilapidated adjoined by other buildings that were similarly decrepit. We entered into the lobby and I felt like I was in a movie, as the apartment complex looked like a crack-house with holes in the walls, bugs crawling on the walls, broken doors, and long dark hallways. It seemed less like a place that someone would live and more likely a scene out of NYPD blue.

We made our way to her floor and walked up to her door. I knocked on the door. I her a shrill voice respond, who is it? The door opened slightly, and I saw her. She looked at me clearly bothered that I had disturbed her, I said, "hello, are you Joann Moore", she said yes, I said I am your son. With a look of rage in her eyes, she screamed at the top of her lungs, a bloodcurdling scream, and slammed the door in my face. The exchange was so abrupt and powerful that we were terrified. The combination of the surroundings and the response was mortifying, so we ran down the hall, shocked, laughing uncomfortably, and emotionally drained. That was the first time I met Joann.

The experience meeting Joann was about as bad as it could have been. There was no happy ending, no new relationship, no positive news to report. Despite this, while I was hurriedly making my way down the hall, I felt the feeling of a physical weight being lifted off of my shoulders – an immense sense of relief. I had realized the burdened I had been carrying my whole life, the burden of rejection. Before then, I had been unaware how deeply I had felt this and how heavy the burden was, until the burden was lifted. In that moment, I knew that Joann had made the right decision for us, there was no possible way should have cared for anyone. It was clear at that time that her declining mental health had only intensified in the twenty-some years following our adoption, Joann was a vestige of herself.

A number of months after my initial meeting with Joann, I felt a sense that I had left too early. I felt that I should have tried harder to talk with her and I didn't want to live with that regret. I decided that I would try again to meet Joann. I made my way back down to San Francisco to see her. I walked down the same long, dark hallway and found her apartment. I knocked on the door. She cracked the door open and said to me, "who are you and what do you want?" I told her I was her son, that she had given birth to twins and that I had been searching for her. She looked at me with an intense stare, looking at my facial features to see me closely. I waited anxiously for her to say something. Then, with not a moment's notice she slammed the door in my face. I stood there for a moment, a little dismayed. However, unlike the first exchange, I wasn't going to let the moment go by. I pulled out a piece of paper and tore off part of it. I wrote on it, "I am your son." I slipped the note under her door. I waited, and waited, wondering if she would write back. Then, I saw an edge of a piece of paper being slipped back through. On it, in response to my statement she wrote "you are? I thought you were."

I was internally exploding with joy that she recognized who I was. I was excited that she had written "I thought you were" and I sensed that this was a moment for her as well. I recognized in that moment that I had a window to communicate with Joann, and that I had better ask anything I wanted to know because I might not get the chance again. So, my attention shifted to determining whether there were any more siblings beyond my twin brother and our newly united sister. I wrote, "do I have any brothers or sisters?" I slipped the note back underneath the door. Very quickly I heard writing and began to see the white edge of the paper being pushed back to me. The response simply said, "yes." Knowing that finding them would require some identifiable information I wrote "what are their names?" I pushed the note through the bottom of the door and waited. This time there was not a quick response. Several seconds went by, then several more. Then I heard writing and saw the note come back. It said the name "Dawn" near the word sister beneath my question. I immediately wrote on the note "What hospital was she born at?" I slipped the note through the door but there was no response. I tried sending more notes through the door, but the responses stopped coming. That exchange was the most meaningful exchange I was ever able to have with Joann.

A number of months later, I went to find Joann again. I went to her apartment and she was not there. I started asking around to see if anyone knew her. I spent half an hour or so asking people if they knew her but no one seemed to. Then, I met a gentleman who lived in the same apartment building, he said that he didn't know her well but knew that everyone called her "the bag lady", a common reference for a homeless woman who has all of her belongings in shopping bags. However, he noted something that was interesting, he said "yeah they call her that because she always has a bag full of books." In further conversation, I learned that she would wake every morning and go to the law library. There she would get a bag full of books, go back to her apartment and read all day and night. Then, the next morning she would repeat the same routine, day after day. Clearly, Joann was both brilliant yet mentally savaged.

A few weeks later, I met Joann for the third time. The meeting was very short, similar to the first encounter. I knocked on the door, she opened up and was coughing. She was visibly ill and had blood dripping from her mouth. She told me to go away and closed the door as she began coughing even harder. I knocked a few times after that. But there was no response and I could sense that she was standing still to avoid making noise with the hope that I would leave. So, I left without pressing further. In some ways, I wish I had. Unfortunately, that was the last time that I would see Joann. She would later die from a heart attack on the steps of the law library carrying a bag of books. Though I never had the kind of interactions with her that I hoped I would, I did have one clear takeaway – her giving us up for adoption was an act of love.

REFERENCES

American Civil Liberties Union (ACLU). (2014a). *United States' compliance with the International Convention on the Elimination of All Forms of Racial Discrimination.* New York, NY: Author.

American Civil Liberties Union (ACLU). (2014b). *Written submission of the American Civil Liberties Union on racial disparities in sentencing: Hearing on reports of racism in the justice system of the United States.* New York, NY: Author.

American Civil Liberties Union (ACLU). (2015). *Picking up the pieces: A Minneapolis case study.* New York, NY: Author.

Allen, Q. (2010). Racial microaggressions: The schooling experiences of Black middle-class males in Arizona's secondary schools. *Journal of African American Males in Education, 1*(2), 125-143. Retrieved from https://digitalcommons.chapman.edu/education_articles/24/

American Psychological Association (APA). (2008). *Are zero tolerance policies effective in the schools?* Washington, DC: APA Zero Tolerance Taskforce.

Araújo, M., & Maeso, S. R. (2012). History textbooks, racism and the critique of Eurocentrism: Beyond rectification or compensation. *Ethnic and Racial Studies, 35,* 1266-1286. doi:10.1080/01419870.2011.600767

Auerbach, C., & Silverstein, L. B. (2003). *Qualitative data: An introduction to coding and analysis.* New York: New York University.

Baumeister, R. F., Bratslavsky, E., Finkenauer, C., & Vohs, K. D. (2001). Bad is stronger than good. *Review of General Psychology, 5,* 323-370. doi:10.1037//1089-2680.5.4.323

Bensimon, E. M. (2007). The underestimated significance of practitioner knowledge in the scholarship on student success. *Review of Higher Education, 30,* 441-469. doi:10.1353/rhe.2007.0032

Bernstein, R. (2017, July 26). Let Black kids just be kids. *The New York Times.* Retrieved from https://www.nytimes.com/2017/07/26/opinion/black-kids-discrimination.html

Bogle, D. (2001). *Toms, coons, mulattoes, mammies, and bucks: An interpretive history of Blacks in American films.* New York, NY: Bloomsbury Academic.

Bonner, F. A., Jennings, M. E., Marbley, A. F., & Brown, L. A. (2008). Capitalizing on leadership capacity: Gifted African American males in high school. *Roeper Review, 30,* 93-103. doi:10.1080/02783190801954965

Boroff, D. (2017). SEE IT: Cops forcefully arrest black Northwestern grad student. *New York Daily News.* Retrieved from http://www.nydailynews.com/news/national/cops-force-arrest-black-northwestern-grad-student-article-1.2945759

Bridges, T. (2011). Towards a pedagogy of hip hop in urban teacher education. *Journal of Negro Education, 80,* 325-338. Retrieved from http://www.jstor.org/stable/41341137

Bui, Q., & Cox, A. (2016). Surprising new evidence shows bias in police use of force but not in shootings. *The New York Times.* Retrieved from https://www.nytimes.com/2016/07/12/upshot/surprising-new-evidence-shows-bias-in-police-use-of-force-but-not-in-shootings.html

Bureau of Justice Statistics. (2011). *Police-public contact survey (PPCS).* Washington, DC: Author.

Bush, L., & Bush, E. C. (2013). Introducing African American male theory (AAMT). *Journal of African American Males in Education, 4*(1), 6-17. Retrieved from https://www.issuelab.org/resources/22925/22925.pdf

California Department of Justice. (2014). *Juvenile justice in California.* Sacramento, CA: Author. Retrieved from https://oag.ca.gov/sites/all/files/agweb/pdfs/cjsc/publications/misc/jj14/preface.pdf

References

Chenoweth, E. (2014). Civil resistance: Reflections on an idea whose time has come. *Global Governance, 20*, 351-358. doi:10.5555/1075-2846-20.3.351

Clawson, R. A. (2002). Poor people, Black faces: The portrayal of poverty in economics textbooks. *Journal of Black Studies, 32*, 352-361. doi:10.1177/002193470203200305

Clinton, H. (1996). *Campaign for crime control bill.* Keene State University, Keene, NH. Retrieved from https://www.c-span.org/video/?69606-1/mrs-clinton-campaign-speech

Collins, J., & Hebert, T. (2008). Race and gender images in psychology textbooks. *Race, Gender & Class, 15*, 300-307. Retrieved from http://www.jstor.org/stable/41674666

Crockett, S. A., Jr. (2015). 10 arrested during RI high school protest after video shows teen slammed by cop. *The Root.* Retrieved from https://www.theroot.com/10-arrested-during-ri-high-school-protest-after-video-s-1790861440

Curran, F. C. (2017). The law, policy, and portrayal of zero tolerance school discipline: Examining prevalence and characteristics across levels of governance and school districts. *Educational Policy.* doi:10.1177%2F0895904817691840

Dancy, T. E. (2014). (Un)doing hegemony in education: Disrupting school-to-prison pipelines for Black males. *Equity & Excellence in Education, 47*, 476-493. doi:10.1080/10665684.2014.959271

Davis, J. E. (1994). College in black and white: Campus environment and academic achievement of African American males. *Journal of Negro Education, 63*, 620-633. Retrieved from http://www.jstor.org/stable/2967299

Davis, J. E. (2003). Early schooling and academic achievement of African American males. *Urban Education, 38*, 515-537. doi:10.1177/0042085903256220

Davis, K., & Littlefield, D. (2017, January 10). Dumanis rules El Cajon police shooting of Alfred Olango justified. *The San Diego Union-Tribune.* Retrieved from http://www.sandiegouniontribune.com/news/courts/sd-me-olango-ruling-20170109-story.html

Delgado, R., & Stefancic, J. (2017). *Critical race theory: An introduction.* New York: New York University Press.

Digest of Education Statistics (2015). *Table 233.70. Percentage of public schools with one or more full-time or part-time security staff present at least once a week, by selected school characteristics: 2005-06 through 2013-14.* Washington, DC: Author.

Dilulio, J. J., Jr. (1995, November 27). The coming of the super—predators. *The Weekly Standard.* Retrieved from http://www.weeklystandard.com/the-coming-of-the-super-predators/article/8160

Dixon, T. F., Jr. (1905). *The clansman: An historical romance of the Ku Klux Klan.* New York, NY: Routledge.

Duckworth, A. (2016). *Grit: The power of passion and perseverance.* New York, NY: Scribner.

Dunham, R. G., & Alpert, G. P. (2015). *Critical issues in policing: Contemporary readings.* Long Grove, IL: Waveland Press.

Education Trust-West. (2015). *Black minds matter: Supporting the educational success of Black children in California.* Oakland, CA: Author.

Essien, I. R. (2012). *Presentation on racial microaggressions in early childhood education.* San Diego, CA: Early Childhood Completion Program.

Essien, I. R., & Wood, J. L. (2018a, November 4). *Pathologizing culture in early childhood education: Illuminating microaggressions from the narratives of Black children.* Paper presented to the National Call of the Moms of Black Boys United.

Essien, I. R., & Wood, J. L. (2018b, November 18). *Ascriptions of intelligence and disregard: Examining Black male children in early childhood education* [PowerPoint]. Paper presented to the National Call of the Moms of Black Boys United.

References

Fain, K. (2015). *Black Hollywood: From butlers to superheroes, the changing role of African American men in the movies.* Santa Barbara, CA: ABC-CLIO.

Ferguson, A. A. (2010). *Bad boys: Public schools in the making of black masculinity.* Ann Arbor: University of Michigan Press.

Ford, D. Y., & Moore, J. L. (2013). Understanding and reversing underachievement, low achievement, and achievement gaps among high-ability African American males in urban school contexts. *The Urban Review, 45*, 399-415. doi:10.1007%2Fs11256-013-0256-3

Ford, D. Y., & Harris, J. J., III. (1997). A study of the racial identity and achievement of Black males and females. *Roeper Review, 20*(2), 105-110.

Freire, P. (1970). *Pedagogy of the oppressed.* New York, NY: Continuum.

Gilliam, W. S., Maupin, A. N., Reyes, C. R., Accavitti, M., & Shic, F. (2016). *Do early educators' biases regarded sex and race relate to behavior expectations and recommendations of preschool expulsions and suspensions?* New Haven, CT: Yale University Child Study Center.

Goff, P. A., Jackson, M. C., Di Leone, B. A. L., Culotta, C. M., & DiTomasso, N. A. (2014). The essence of innocence: Consequences of dehumanizing Black children. *Journal of Personality and Social Psychology, 106*, 526-545. doi:10.1037/a0035663

Griffith, D. W. (Producer & Director) (1915). *The birth of a nation* [Motion picture]. United States: Epoch Producing Co.

Hackman, R. (2016, July 12). 'It's like we're seen as animals': Black men on their vulnerability and resilience. *The Guardian.* Retrieved from https://www.theguardian.com/world/2016/jul/12/black-men-america-violence-vulnerable-detroit

Hanson, H. (2017). Video shows cop in school grabbing teen by neck, slamming him to floor. *Huffington Post.* Retrieved from https://www.huffingtonpost.com/entry/round-rock-high-school-cop-grabs-student-neck_us_561a6560e4b0dbb8000ee689

Harper, S. R. (2009). Niggers no more: A critical race counternarrative on Black male student achievement at predominantly White colleges and universities. *International Journal of Qualitative Studies in Education, 22*, 697-712. doi:10.1080/09518390903333889

Harper, S. R. (2014). (Re)setting the agenda for college men of color: Lessons learned from a 15-year movement to improve Black male student success. In R. A. Williams (Ed.), *Men of color in higher education: New foundations for developing models for success* (pp. 116-143). Sterling, VA: Stylus.

Harper, S. R., & Wood, J. L. (Eds.). (2015). *Advancing Black male student success: From preschool through PhD.* Sterling, VA: Stylus.

Harris, F., III, & Harper, S. R. (2008). Masculinities go to community college: Understanding male identity socialization and gender role conflict. *New Directions for Community Colleges, 2008*(142), 25-35.

Horning, K. T. (2017). *Publishing statistics on children's books about people of color and first/native nations and by people of color and first/native nations -authors and illustrators.* Madison, WI: Cooperative Children's Book Center School of Education.

Howard, T. C. (2013a). How does it feel to be a problem? Black male students, schools, and learning in enhancing the knowledge base to disrupt deficit frameworks. *Review of Research in Education, 37*(1), 54-86. doi:10.3102/0091732X12462985

Howard, T. C. (2013b). *Black male (d): Peril and promise in the education of African American males.* New York, NY: Teachers College Press.

Howard, T. C. (2016). Why Black lives (and minds) matter: Race, freedom schools & the quest for educational equity. *Journal of Negro Education, 85*, 101-113. doi:10.7709/jnegroeducation.85.2.0101

Hughes, L. (1967). *The panther & the lash: Poems of our times.* New York, NY: Vintage.

References

Judge, M. (2017), Video appears to show school-resource officer placing student in choke hold for no reason. *The Root.* Retrieved from https://www.theroot.com/surveillance-video-shows-school-resource-officer-placin-1794902013

Kahn, A., & Kirk, C. (2015). What it's like to be Black in the criminal justice system: These eight charts suggest that there are racial disparities at every phase of the justice system. *The Slate.* Retrieved from http://www.slate.com/articles/news_and_politics/crime/2015/08/racial_disparities_in_the_criminal_justice_system_eight_charts_illustrating.html

Kinsler, J. (2011). Understanding the Black–White school discipline gap. *Economics of Education Review, 30,* 1370-1383. doi:10.1016/j.econedurev.2011.07.004

Kuh, G. D. (2003). What we're learning about student engagement from NSSE: Benchmarks for effective educational practices. *Change: The Magazine of Higher Learning, 35*(2), 24-32. doi:10.1080/00091380309604090

Kutateladze, B. L., & Andiloro, N. R. (2014). *Prosecution and racial justice in New York County* [Technical report]. Washington, DC: U.S. Department of Justice.

Ladson-Billings, G. (1995). Toward a theory of culturally relevant pedagogy. *American Educational Research Journal, 32,* 465-491. doi:10.3102/00028312032003465

Ladson Billings, G. (2011). Boyz to men? Teaching to restore Black boys' childhood. *Race Ethnicity and Education, 14*(1), 7-15. doi:10.1080/13613324.2011.531977

Lowery, W., & Scruggs, A. (2015, December 2). Cleveland officers say Tamir Rice reached into waistband and pulled toy gun before one of them shot him. *The Washington Post.* Retrieved from https://www.washingtonpost.com/news/post-nation/wp/2015/12/01/cleveland-officers-say-tamir-rice-reached-into-waistband-and-pulled-toy-gun-before-one-of-them-shot-him/?utm_term=.3b78b531ff6b

Mannix, A. (2016). Police audio: Officer stopped Philando Castile on robbery suspicion: Police recording doesn't cover shooting itself. *StarTribune.* Retrieved from http://www.startribune.com/police-audio-officer-stopped-philando-castile-on-robbery-suspicion/386344001/#1

McAdoo, H. P. (Ed.). (2007). *Black families.* Los Angeles, CA: Sage.

Modell, S. J., & Cropp, D. (2007). Police officers and disability: Perceptions and attitudes. *Intellectual and Developmental Disabilities, 45*(1), 60-63. doi:10.1352/1934-9556(2007)45[60:POADPA]2.0.CO;2

National Institute of Justice. (2005). *Mapping crime: Understanding hot spots.* Washington, DC: U.S. Department of Justice, Office of Justice Programs. Retrieved from https://www.ncjrs.gov/pdffiles1/nij/209393.pdf

New York Civil Liberties Union (2011). *Stop and frisk 2011.* New York, NY: Author.

New York Times Editorial Board (2016, December 17). Unequal sentences for Blacks and Whites. *The New York Times.* Retrieved from https://www.nytimes.com/2016/12/17/opinion/sunday/unequal-sentences-for-blacks-and-whites.html?smid=tw-share

Noguchi, K., Kamada, A., & Shrira, I. (2014). Cultural differences in the primacy effect for person perception. *International Journal of Psychology, 49,* 208-210. doi:10.1002/ijop.12019

Noguera, P. A. (2003). The trouble with Black boys: The role and influence of environmental and cultural factors on the academic performance of African American males. *Urban Education, 38,* 431-459. doi:10.1177/0042085903038004005

The Pew Charitable Trusts. (2008). *One in 100: Behind bars in America 2008.* Retrieved from http://www.pewtrusts.org/en/research-and-analysis/reports/2008/02/28/one-in-100-behind-bars-in-america-2008

References

Pewewardy, C. (1993). Culturally responsible pedagogy in action: An American Indian magnet school. In E. Hollins, J. King, & W. Hayman (Eds.), *Teaching diverse populations: Formulating a knowledge base* (pp. 77-92). Albany: State University of New York.

Rendón, L. I. (1994). Validating culturally diverse students: Toward a new model of learning and student development. *Innovative Higher Education, 19*(1), 33-51. doi:10.1007/BF01191156

Roufa, T. (2018, January 18). Guard or warriors? The changing role of law enforcement. *The Balance.* Retrieved from https://www.thebalance.com/law-enforcement-changing-role-974558

Sadler, M. S., Correll, J., Park, B., & Judd, C. M. (2012). The world is not black and white: Racial bias in the decision to shoot in a multiethnic context. *Journal of Social Issues, 68*, 286-313. doi:10.1111/j.1540-4560.2012.01749.x

Sanchez, C. G., & Rosenbaum, D. P. (2011). Racialized policing: Officers' voices on policing Latino and African American neighborhoods. *Journal of Ethnicity in Criminal Justice, 9*, 152-178. doi:10.1080/15377938.2011.566821

Sanford, N. (1962). The developmental status of freshman. In N. Sanford (Ed.), *The American college: A psychological and social interpretation of the higher learning* (pp. 253-282). New York, NY: John Wiley and Sons.

The Sentencing Project (2013). *Report of the Sentencing Project to the United Nations Human Rights Committee: Regarding racial disparities in the United States criminal justice system.* Washington, DC: Author. Retrieved from http://sentencingproject.org/wp-content/uploads/2015/12/Race-and-Justice-Shadow-Report-ICCPR.pdf

Steele, C. M. (1997). A threat in the air: How stereotypes shape intellectual identity and performance. *American Psychologist, 52*, 613-629. doi:10.1037/0003-066X.52.6.613

Strayhorn, T. L., & Tillman-Kelly, D. L. (2013). Queering masculinity: Manhood and Black gay men in college. *Spectrum: A Journal on Black Men, 1*(2), 83-110. doi:10.2979/spectrum.1.2.83

Sue, D. W., Capodilupo, C. M., Torino, G. C., Bucceri, J. M., Holder, A., Nadal, K. L., & Esquilin, M. (2007). Racial microaggressions in everyday life: Implications for clinical practice. *American Psychologist, 62*, 271-286. doi:10.1037/0003-066X.62.4.271

TED. (2014). The power of believing that you can improve [Video file]. *YouTube.* Retrieved from https://www.youtube.com/watch?v=_X0mgOOSpLU

Thacher, D. E. (2014). Order maintenance policing. In M. D. Reisig & R. J. Kane (Ed.), *The Oxford handbook of police and policing* (pp. 122-147). Oxford, England: Oxford University Press.

Thistle, S. (2006). *From marriage to the market: The transformation of women's lives and work.* Oakland: University of California Press.

Turner, C. S. V. (1994). Guests in someone else's house: Students of color. *Review of Higher Education, 17*, 355-370. doi:10.1353/rhe.1994.0008

U.S. Office of Civil Rights. (2014a). *Civil rights data collection: Data snapshot: Early childhood education.* Washington, DC: Author. Retrieved from https://www2.ed.gov/about/offices/list/ocr/docs/crdc-early-learning-snapshot.pdf

U.S. Office of Civil Rights. (2014b). *Civil rights data collection: Data snapshot: Discipline.* Washington, DC: Author. Retrieved from https://ocrdata.ed.gov/downloads/crdc-school-discipline-snapshot.pdf

U.S. Sentencing Commission. (2011). *Chapter 7: Statistical overview of mandatory minimum penalties.* Washington, DC: Author. Retrieved from https://www.ussc.gov/sites/default/files/pdf/news/congressional-testimony-and-reports/mandatory-minimum-penalties/20111031-rtc-pdf/Chapter_07.pdf

Wilson, J. Q., & Kelling, G. L. (1982). Broken windows. *Atlantic Monthly, 249*(3), 29-38. Retrieved from http://www.lantm.lth.se/fileadmin/fastighetsvetenskap/utbildning/Fastighetsvaerderingssystem/BrokenWindowTheory.pdf

References

Wood, J. L. (2014). Apprehension to engagement in the classroom: Perceptions of Black males in the community college. *International Journal of Qualitative Studies in Education, 27*, 785-803. doi:10.108 0/09518398.2014.901575

Wood, J. L. (2017, November 7). Black minds matter – Week 3, featuring Donna Y. Ford and Fred A. Bonner III [Video file]. *YouTube*. Retrieved from https://www.youtube.com/watch?v=x_rZcZD1Jlg&t=2732s

Wood, J. L., Essien, I., & Blevins, D. (2017). Black males in kindergarten: The effect of social skills on close and conflictual relationships with teachers. *Journal of African American Males in Education, 8*(2), 30-50. Retrieved from http://journalofafricanamericanmales.com/wp-content/uploads/2017/12/4-Wood-et-al-2017-Black-Males-in-Kindergarten.pdf

Wood, J. L., & Harris, F., III. (2016). Too smart to succeed, too good to win: The plight of Black professionals and students. *Huffington Post*. Retrieved from https://www.huffingtonpost.com/entry/too-smart-to-succeed-too-good-to-win-the-plight_us_58275e9de4b02b1f5257a329

Wood, J. L., Harris, F., III, & White (2015). *Teaching men of color in the community college: A guidebook*. San Diego, CA: Lawndale Hill.

Wood, J. L., & Harris, F., III. (2017a). *Supporting men of color in the community college: A guidebook*. San Diego, CA: Lawndale Hill.

Wood, J. L., & Harris, F., III. (2017b). *Teaching boys and young men of color: A guidebook*. San Diego, CA: Lawndale Hill.

Wood, J. L., Harris, F., III, & Howard, T. C. (2018). *GET OUT: Black male suspensions in California public schools*. San Diego, CA: Community College Equity Assessment Lab and UCLA Black Male Institute.

Wood, L. J., & Hilton, A. A. (2013). Moral choices: Towards a conceptual model of black male moral development (BMMD). *Western Journal of Black Studies, 37*(1), 14-27.

Wood, J. L., Hilton, A. A., & Hicks, T. (2014). Motivational factors for academic success: Perspectives of African American males in the community college. *National Journal of Urban Education & Practice, 7,* 247-265.

Woodson, A. N. (2015). "What you supposed to know": Urban Black students' perspectives on history textbooks. *Journal of Urban Learning Teaching and Research, 11,* 57-65.

APPENDIX

20 Must Read Works for Educators of Black Boys and Men

Bonner, F. A., Jennings, M. E., Marbley, A. F., & Brown, L. A. (2008). Capitalizing on leadership capacity: Gifted African American males in high school. *Roeper Review, 30,* 93-103. doi:10.1080/02783190801954965

Dancy, T. E. (2014). (Un)doing hegemony in education: Disrupting school-to-prison pipelines for Black males. *Equity & Excellence in Education, 47,* 476-493. doi:10.1080/10665684.2014.959271

Davis, J. E. (1994). College in Black and White: Campus environment and academic achievement of African American males. *Journal of Negro Education, 63,* 620-633. doi:10.2307/2967299

Ford, D. Y., & Moore, J. L. (2013). Understanding and reversing underachievement, low achievement, and achievement gaps among high-ability African American males in urban school contexts. *The Urban Review, 45,* 399-415. doi:10.1007/s11256-013-0256-3

Harper, S. R. (2009). Niggers no more: A critical race counternarrative on Black male student achievement at predominantly White colleges and universities. *International Journal of Qualitative Studies in Education, 22,* 697-712. doi:10.1080/09518390903333889

Harper, S. R. (2014). (Re)setting the agenda for college men of color: Lessons learned from a 15-year movement to improve Black male student success. In R. A. Williams (Ed.), *Men of color in higher education: New foundations for developing models for success* (pp. 116-143). Sterling, VA: Stylus.

Harris, F., III, Palmer, R. T., & Struve, L. E. (2011). "Cool posing" on campus: A qualitative study of masculinities and gender expression among Black men at a private research institution. *Journal of Negro Education, 80,* 47-62. Retrieved from http://www.jstor.org/stable/41341105

Howard, T. C. (2016). Why Black lives (and minds) matter: Race, freedom schools & the quest for educational equity. *Journal of Negro Education, 85*, 101-113. doi:10.7709/jnegroeducation.85.2.0101

Howard, T. C., Douglass, T., & Warren, C. (2016). "What works?" Recommendations in transformation of Black male educational outcomes. *Teachers College Record, 118*(6), 1-10. Retrieved from https://www.researchgate.net/publication/306013047_What_Works_Recommendations_on_Improving_Academic_Experiences_and_Outcomes_for_Black_Males

Ladson Billings, G. (2011). Boyz to men? Teaching to restore Black boys' childhood. *Race Ethnicity and Education, 14*(1), 7-15. doi:10.1080/13613324.2011.531977

Moore, J. L., III, Madison-Colmore, O., & Smith, D. M. (2003). The prove-them-wrong syndrome: Voices from unheard African-American males in engineering disciplines. *Journal of Men's Studies, 12*(1), 61-73. doi:10.3149/jms.1201.61

Noguera, P. A. (2003). The trouble with Black boys: The role and influence of environmental and cultural factors on the academic performance of African American males. *Urban Education, 38*, 431-459. doi:10.1177/0042085903038004005

Palmer, R. T., Davis, R. J., & Hilton, A. A. (2009). Exploring challenges that threaten to impede the academic success of academically underprepared Black males at an HBCU. *Journal of College Student Development, 50*, 429-445. doi:10.1353/csd.0.0078

Sealey-Ruiz, Y., & Lewis, C. (2013). Letters to our teachers: Black and Latino males write about race in the urban English classroom. In J. Landsman (Ed.), *Talking about race: Alleviating the fear* (pp. 274-290). Sterling, VA: Stylus.

Smith, W. A., Allen, W. R, & Danley, L. L. (2007). "Assume the position . . . you fit the description": Psychosocial experiences and racial battle fatigue among African American male college students. *American Behavioral Scientist, 51*, 551-578. doi:10.1177/0002764207307742

Appendix

Strayhorn, T. L., & Tillman-Kelly, D. L. (2013). Queering masculinity: Manhood and Black gay men in college. *Spectrum: A Journal on Black Men, 1*, 83-110. doi:10.2979/spectrum.1.2.83

Tatum, A. W. (2008). Toward a more anatomically complete model of literacy instruction: A focus on African American male adolescents and texts. *Harvard Educational Review, 78*, 155-180. doi:10.17763/haer.78.1.6852t5065w30h449

Toldson, I. A., Sutton, R. M., & Brown, R. L. F. (2012). Preventing delinquency and promoting academic success among school-age African American males. *Journal of African American Males in Education, 3*(1), 12-27. Retrieved from http://diversity.utexas.edu/aamri/wp-content/uploads/2015/02/Preventing-Delinquency-pdf..pdf

Wood, J. L. (2014). Apprehension to engagement in the classroom: Perceptions of Black males in the community college. *International Journal of Qualitative Studies in Education, 27*, 785-803. doi:10.1080/09518398.2014.901575

Wood, J. L., & Essien-Wood, I. (2012). Capital identity projection: Understanding the psychosocial effects of capitalism on Black male community college students. *Journal of Economic Psychology, 33*, 984-995. doi:10.1016/j.joep.2012.06.001